WINGS ACROSS AMERICA

WINGS ACROSS AMERICA

150 OUTRAGEOUSLY DELICIOUS CHICKEN-WING RECIPES

Armand C. Vanderstigchel

A Birch Lane Press Book
Published by Carol Publishing Group

A Birch Lane Press Book
Published by Carol Publishing Group
Birch Lane Press is a registered trademark of Carol Communications, Inc.

Editorial, sales and distribution, rights and permissions inquiries should be addressed to Carol Publishing Group, 120 Enterprise Avenue, Secaucus, NJ 07094.

In Canada: Canadian Manda Group, One Atlantic Avenue, Suite 105, Toronto, Ontario M6K 3E7

Carol Publishing books may be purchased in bulk at special discounts for sales promotion, fund-raising, or educational purposes. Special editions can be created to specifications. For details, contact Special Sales Department, 120 Enterprise Avenue, Secaucus, NJ 07094.

Designed by Tevonian Design

Manufactured in the United States of America

10 9 8 7 6 5 4 3 2 1

Library of Congress Cataloging-in-Publication Data

Vanderstigchel, Armand C.
    Wings across America : 150 outrageously delicious chicken-wing
recipes / Armand C. Vanderstigchel
        p.   cm.
    "A Birch Lane Press book."
    Includes index.
    ISBN 1-55972-456-0 (hc.)
    1. Cookery (Chicken)   2. Cookery, American.   I. Title.
TX750.5C45V36   1999
641.6'65—dc21   98-50689
                                                               CIP

This book is dedicated to the people who have helped me make this book a reality. I also dedicate this book to the memory of Charlotte Morrison, Henrietta Birkel, and Robinetta Birkel. You are missed.

CONTENTS

ACKNOWLEDGMENTS

Writing a cookbook can be as thrilling and scary as a roller-coaster ride. To keep the coaster on the tracks you sometimes need to call on your network of friends to keep things going smoothly.

Thanks to "Super Agent" B. K. Nelson, who was the backbone of this project. Your amazing energy, dedication, and belief in me are truly appreciated. You made this crazy idea work and got another author into the world of publishing. I would also like to thank my editor, Lynda Dickey, and all the wonderful people at Carol Publishing for their involvement in this book. Without all of your efforts I would be nowhere.

Very special thanks to my friend and business partner Robert Birkel Jr., who toiled with me on our first book, *The Adirondack Cookbook.* I would also like to thank Michael Morrison, a brother in arms, who has battled beside me throughout our years in the restaurant business. He has always been there when needed to test another recipe.

Thanks to my family and friends: my parents and family in Holland and Germany; Pa Morrison, Pa, Brian, Jean and Jacky Birkel, Glenn and Laurie Morrison, Mom Miller, and my cooking-class friends, Kathy Deegan, Alex Cordero, Jeff Mucilio, Willy and Mom Kerrigan, Paulino Keyes, Lynn Connors, Pam and Peter Marino, Salomon Caldeira, Paul and Marie at Skippers, Brian Roesch, Tommy and Maria Dimonti, Steven Carroll, Linda Ringhouse at Dog and the Duck in Sayville, New York, Lessings Inc., Rivervieuw Restaurant, Oakdale, New York, Jimmy and Laura Hahn, John Schlenke, Chef Hosè, Jack Lessing, and Smitty Lessing.

Many thanks to these restaurants and hot-sauce companies: Ivano and Joanne at the Anchor Bar in Buffalo, New York; Patrica and Cedric Singleterry at Wings of Glory in Dallas; the Spagnoli family at Yak-Zies in Chicago; Melina, Steve, and Greg at Pluck U in New York City; the Baja Grill in East Northport, New York; Larry at Totally Wings in Huntington, New York; Jill, Donna, and Stacy at the Bender Agency for Frank's Red Hot Sauce; Tabasco; Tahiti Joe; Richard Torte at the Inn at Saratoga, New York; and *Chile Pepper* magazine, John Tuscan of Schreiber Spices.

For artwork, thanks to Ron Alcaris, Paulino Keyes, Alex Cordes and Elite Photo, and the Drawing Board Studios. Also Jim Connors (Internet) and Al Rossino at the Hot Shoppe, Syracuse, New York, for the hot-sauce connection.

Very special thanks to Paul Prudhomme, Richard Simmons, Larry Forgione, Charlie Trotter, Fritz Sonnenschmidt at CIA, John McBride, Tommy Tang, and Doug Feindt at Captain Redbeard's.

INTRODUCTION

One hundred and fifty ways to cook chicken wings? Well, why not? Chicken wings are more popular than ever; they now rank among America's favorite appetizer choices. They taste great and make perfect finger food!

And what makes them taste so great? Have you ever thought about the difference in taste between a cut of prime rib on the bone and a boneless cut? Or a juicy veal osso buco versus veal cutlet scallopini? In both cases, it's the bone that provides extra flavor during the cooking process. That's why wings taste so great next to a neutral-flavored boneless chicken breast.

My love for wings sprouted from a curiosity generated by hearing so much about them, and the delicious aroma of freshly prepared wings being carried through dining rooms across the country to hungry diners. After I got my first taste of them, I was hooked!

My new passion prompted me to experiment with different ways of preparing them. Soon I had created over one hundred new recipes. A hobby became an obsession—an obsession became an idea—an idea became a book.

I hope that you, whether wing lover, chef, cook, restaurateur, or "wing virgin," will rise to the challenge presented here and try some of these recipes compiled for you. Also included are step-by-step basics, side dishes, humor, history, and much more. Dig in!

WINGS ACROSS AMERICA

WING BASICS

n this chapter, I will supply you with the little secrets that go into making perfect wings. I have gathered these secrets from my own experience as well as from professional wing cooks.

PURCHASING FRESH WINGS

Assure yourself of buying the freshest-quality wings by doing the following:

- Check the expiration date on the package. Make sure it's not past!
- Make sure the wings are USDA Grade A.
- Check the color of the wings; it should be bright yellow or white. A grayish color is a no-no!
- Very little blood should have accumulated on the bottom of the package.
- Look for meaty wings; don't pay for bones.
- If you have access to a local butcher, try ordering wings from him or her. Small private shops survive on their reputation for freshness.

PURCHASING FROZEN WINGS

Frozen wings can be purchased in bulk bags, cleaned, trimmed, and ready for use. The price is often quite low. If frozen wings are more convenient for you, follow these steps when you thaw them:

- Keep the wings frozen until the day before you intend to use them.

- Remove the wings from the bag and set them on a wire oven rack placed on a baking sheet with a rim.
- Place the sheet in the refrigerator. As the wings thaw, the liquids will drip onto the baking sheet; be sure to drain this excess water from the sheet during the thawing process.
- Once the wings are thawed, remove them from the rack. Pat them dry with a clean kitchen towel before cooking.

HANDLING WINGS WITH CARE

To avoid food poisoning and salmonella, it's important to not only buy the freshest wings possible but also adhere to the following safety guidelines:

- Wash your hands with hot water and soap before *and* after handling chicken wings.
- Clean the preparation area and cutting board with hot water and a dash of bleach before and after wing preparation.
- Raw wings should be cut on an acrylic or hard plastic cutting board rather than one made of wood or another porous material.
- Always thaw and marinate wings in the refrigerator.
- Refrigerate wings immediately after purchase and use them within two days. If this is not possible, place them in a sealed freezer bag and freeze them. Discard them if they aren't used within six months.

WING QUANTITIES

A good rule of thumb is that there are about ten untrimmed wings or twenty trimmed wings in two pounds, depending on the wing size. Twenty wings will make about four appetizer-sized servings (five wings per serving) or two main-dish-sized servings (ten wings per serving).

TRIMMING AND SEPARATING WINGS

Wings often cost less per pound if you buy them whole (untrimmed). If you prefer to trim your own, you'll need a sharp ten-inch chef's knife or cleaver (poultry shears also work well), a cutting board or butcher's block, and a moist kitchen towel. Spread the moist towel beneath the cutting board to keep it from slipping. Pat the wings dry; trim one wing at a time, following these instructions:

1. Place the wing on the cutting board as shown, after gently pulling on the different sections of the wing to loosen the joint connections.

2. Using a sharp knife, cut the wing tip off and discard it. You can also remove excess fat and the skin, if desired.

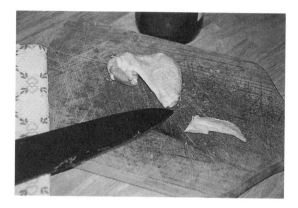

3. Now cut in between the remaining two parts at the joint, resulting in what looks like a miniature drumstick and a winglike small piece. Ta da! You're ready to cook!

COOKING METHODS

FRYING

- Always use clean or filtered soy, canola, or peanut oil. These oils have a high smoking point, which produces crispy wings and leaves no aftertaste.
- The ideal frying temperature is 350° to 375° F. Purchase a frying thermometer for greater temperature accuracy.
- Don't overcrowd the fryer or pan. Too many wings will lower the oil's temperature.
- Make sure the wings are dry to prevent oil spattering.
- Bring the wings to room temperature. Frozen or cold wings will lower the oil's temperature.
- Always use a deep pot when frying on a gas stove to avoid a pan fire.
- Wings are cooked when they are crispy and golden brown, and their internal temperature has reached 170° F. Use a small meat thermometer to check this.

BAKING

- Always preheat the oven fifteen minutes prior to baking.
- Always use a timer to measure cooking time; this way you'll be reminded when the wings are done, in case you get distracted.
- Check the wings every five minutes to prevent sticking or burning.

GRILLING AND BARBECUING

- Preheat the grill forty-five minutes prior to cooking. This will prevent sticking and produce crispier wings.
- Brush the grill with a wire cleaning brush before and after each grilling session to promote better heat distribution.

• Grease the grill with a brush dipped in vegetable oil, or spray with nonstick cooking spray, to prevent sticking. Also, make sure the wings have been marinated or brushed with oil.

• Pay attention to wings that have been marinated in any heavy sugar-based marinade. They tend to burn and stick faster.

• Barbecuing with wood chips instead of charcoal creates a smoky, flavorful wing.

• Lower the temperature (or raise the grill from the coals) once the wings are crispy. Using a meat thermometer, make sure that the internal temperature of the wings is 165° F. If the wings need more time, pull them from the hottest part of the grill to the side to let them finish cooking.

• The "drumstick" part of the wing cooks faster than the wing part. Remove these from the grill first.

SECRETS OF TASTY WINGS

• Always make sure to season your wings with a little salt and pepper if you aren't marinating them. This will bring out more flavor. Add a little cayenne pepper for heat.

• Always use top-quality sauces and the freshest ingredients.

• Marinate wings for more flavor.

COOKING EQUIPMENT

The following equipment may be useful when you cook various chicken-wing recipes.

BAKING DISH. A heavy-duty ceramic or glass dish for oven-baked wings with lots of sauce.

BAKING SHEET. A resilient sheet of nonstick or regular aluminum with a rim.

BASTING BRUSH. For brushing grilled or baked wings with sauce or marinade during the cooking process.

CUTTING BOARD. A board of hard acrylic for cutting and trimming wings and ingredients.

CONDIMENT BOWL. A round or oval glass or ceramic bowl for serving blue cheese or other dips with carrots or celery.

MIXING BOWL. A medium to large bowl in which to toss wings with sauce.

PAELLA PAN. A wide, shallow, two-handled pan for cooking Wing Paella or Wing Fried Rice.

POULTRY SHEARS. Large, sharp scissors for cutting wing tips and in between joints.

SAUCEPAN. For cooking and simmering wing stews.

SAUTÉ PAN. A heavy, stainless-steel, cast-iron, or aluminum pan for efficient browning and pan-frying of wings.

THERMOMETER. An instant-read thermometer for measuring internal temperature. Insert it into the thickest part of the wing.

WIRE BRUSH. A brush with stiff metal bristles designed to clean and brush the grill before and after cooking.

WIRE SPIDER. A large spiderweblike wire spoon useful when fishing wings out of frying oil.

WOK. A deep, round Chinese cooking pan designed for quick, high-heat frying.

THE HISTORY OF "BUFFALO" CHICKEN WINGS

Almost everyone is familiar with the term *Buffalo wings*. Many have enjoyed this dish as a tasty appetizer or even a full meal. But who knows the true story of how Buffalo wings came to be?

According to some, the Buffalo wing was first created at a Buffalo, New York, restaurant called the Anchor Bar, which dates back to the 1920s. Teressa and Frank Bellissimo, an ambitious young couple, opened the Anchor on Canal Street, near Buffalo's waterfront. It was frequented by sailors from ships anchored in Lake Erie.

In 1935 they moved the Anchor to Main Street (where the bar is located to this day). At that time the restaurant was generally known for its Italian food and jazz performances on weekends; owners Frank and Teressa could occasionally be seen on the dance floor.

Then, one enchanted Friday night in 1964, it happened . . . *Buffalo wings were born!*

The couple's son, Don "Rooster" Bellissimo, was working his usual bar shift that evening. It was a busy one, with Teressa working in the kitchen and Frank greeting customers in the restaurant.

Around midnight, a bowling team came into the restaurant to celebrate a recent victory. Dom asked his mother to fix something for the guys. She assured them she would whip something up; however, once in the kitchen, she realized that she had a problem. Because Buffalo had a large Catholic population and there was little demand for meat on Friday, the restaurant hadn't ordered meat that day. This meant no quick hamburgers or steaks. What could she make to satisfy the hungry crowd? Then Teressa remembered that the meat supplier had sent them some chicken wings for stocks and gravies. She had saved them in the refrigerator.

Desperate, she fried the chicken wings in vegetable oil then tossed them with a mixture of Louisiana hot sauce, margarine, and spices. She put the wings on plates with celery and carrot sticks and blue cheese dressing, and served the two heaping platters to her hungry guests. Everyone loved them, and Buffalo chicken wings were born!

After that Friday night, the customers started going crazy. Within a month, word about the new culinary invention had spread around Buffalo. Soon the Anchor was selling four thousand pounds of wings a week!

WINGS ON THE INTERNET

As the popularity of chicken wings grows, more and more sites featuring these treats have sprung up on the Internet. In fact, a recent search using AltaVista's search engine brought up over two thousand matches! Chicken wings and wing recipes are featured in cooking magazine sites, online cookbooks, and recipe databases. Many individuals have posted their favorite recipes and wing restaurants. Hot sauce manufacturers both provide recipes using their products and take orders over the Internet, making that unusual hot sauce easier to obtain.

Here are some of my favorite wing-related sites:

The Wing Thing Web Page: http://members.aol.com/wildrusk/WingThing.html

How Rick Enjoys Wings: http://www.buffnet.net/~johnston/wings/wings.htm

Chicken Wing Central: http://bvsd.k12.co.us/~alums/wings.html

Michael's Buffalo Wing Recipe Archive:http://www.bababooey.com/monkey/wings.html

And, of course . . .

The Anchor Bar Home Page: http://www.buffalowings.com

AMERICAN WING RECIPES

n this chapter, I focus on American-style wings. These recipes have been kept as simple as possible, using ingredients readily found at any supermarket.

Note: These recipes all yield four appetizer-sized servings or two main-dish-sized servings.

ADIRONDACK MAPLE WINGS

☞ **Since** I cowrote *The Adirondack Cookbook,* it was obvious that I create an Adirondack chicken-wing recipe. This one had great public appeal at recent cooking demonstrations. The igniting of the whiskey in the pan is always a great showstopper.

2 tablespoons vegetable oil
20 trimmed and separated
  wings
Pinch each salt and pepper
¼ cup Johnny Walker Black
  Label whiskey

1 cup barbecue sauce (I like
  Bull's Eye)
¼ cup Adirondack or pure
  maple syrup
Dash hot sauce
2 tablespoons (¼ stick)
  unsalted butter

1. In a large skillet, heat the oil over a high flame.

2. Add the wings and sprinkle with salt and pepper. Cook for 10 to 15 minutes or until golden brown, firm, and cooked through.

3. Splash with whiskey, then ignite. To assure a nice flame, the pan must be hot. Once lit, the flame will burn for 30 seconds (don't be afraid; it *will* die out).

4. Add the barbecue sauce, maple syrup, and hot sauce.

5. Simmer for 1 minute. Melt the butter into the sauce.

6. Remove the wings from the skillet and place them in a large bowl. Toss with the sauce until they're completely coated.

BORN ON THE BAYOU WINGS

1 cup all-purpose flour
2 tablespoons cornstarch
2 teaspoons baking powder
1 cup cold water
¼ cup bourbon
1 tablespoon Cajun
  seasoning
¼ teaspoon ground nutmeg
¼ teaspoon ground
  cinnamon

½ teaspoon garlic powder
½ teaspoon onion powder
½ tablespoon sugar
1 teaspoon salt
Oil, for deep-frying
All-purpose flour, for
  breading
20 trimmed and separated
  wings

1. Combine the flour, cornstarch, baking powder, water, bourbon, Cajun seasoning, nutmeg, cinnamon, garlic and onion powders, sugar, and salt in a large mixing bowl. Be careful not to overmix; it weakens the batter, resulting in a poor crust.

2. Heat the oil in a fryer at 350° F, or heat 2 inches of oil in a large, heavy skillet.

3. Lightly coat the wings with flour.

4. Dip the wings into the batter, making sure they're thoroughly coated. (The batter should drip very slowly from each coated wing.)

5. Fry the wings one at a time for 10 to 15 minutes or until they're firm, brown, crispy, and cooked through.

6. Drain on paper towels.

CALIFORNIA AVOCADO WINGS

☞ ❙ know this combination sounds a little unusual, but have courage and try it!

2 tablespoons vegetable oil
20 trimmed and separated
   wings
Dash each salt and pepper
2 large California avocados,
   peeled and pitted
1 small onion, minced
1 garlic clove, minced
⅓ cup whole milk
⅓ cup sour cream
⅛ teaspoon salt

⅛ teaspoon ground black
   pepper
½ teaspoon onion powder
½ teaspoon garlic powder
½ teaspoon ground cumin
2 tablespoons chopped fresh
   cilantro
1 tablespoon fresh lemon
   juice
Dash hot sauce

1. Heat the oil in a large, heavy skillet over a high flame. Add the wings, sprinkling with salt and pepper to seal in their flavor while they brown. Fry the wings for 10 to 12 minutes, or until brown and cooked through. Remove from the heat, set aside, and keep warm.

2. In the meantime, combine the avocados, onion, garlic, milk, sour cream, spices, lemon juice, and hot sauce in a food processor, and pulse until smooth.

3. Combine the cooked wings and the avocado mixture in a large mixing bowl, and toss until the wings are thoroughly coated. Transfer to a platter and serve with tortilla chips.

THE CREAM IS SOUR WINGS

2 tablespoons vegetable oil
20 trimmed and separated
* wings*
Dash each salt and pepper
1 cup sour cream
½ tablespoon fresh lemon
* juice*
¼ cup chopped green
* onions (scallions)*

1 tablespoon chopped fresh
* parsley*
½ tablespoon Dijon mustard
½ tablespoon grated
* horseradish*
½ teaspoon minced fresh
* gingerroot*
⅛ teaspoon cayenne pepper

1. Heat the oil in a large, heavy skillet over a high flame. Add the wings, sprinkling with salt and pepper, and fry for 10 to 12 minutes, or until brown and cooked through. Remove from the heat and keep warm.

2. In a large mixing bowl, combine the sour cream, lemon juice, green onions, parsley, mustard, horseradish, ginger, salt, pepper, and cayenne. Mix well.

3. With tongs, remove the wings from the skillet and place them in the bowl with the sauce. Toss, making sure the wings are thoroughly coated.

DARKEST SECRET WINGS

☞ **It's** quite amazing how delicious and versatile beer is, as it can be used in recipes ranging from appetizers to desserts. Try this wing recipe made with dark beer!

20 trimmed and separated
   wings
2 tablespoons vegetable oil
Dash each salt and pepper
1 leek stem, washed and
   diced fine
½ cup diced onion
4 shallots, chopped fine
½ teaspoon crushed
   caraway seeds (crush
   with a pan)

1 12-ounce bottle dark beer
3 tablespoons light brown
   sugar, packed
½ teaspoon dried thyme
½ teaspoon onion powder
½ teaspoon garlic powder
2 tablespoons (¼ stick)
   unsalted butter

1. In a large, heavy skillet, heat the oil over a high flame.

2. Add the wings. Season with salt and pepper. This will seal in extra flavor while you're browning the wings.

3. Add the leek, onion, shallots, and crushed caraway.

5. Brown and caramelize the mixture for about 3 minutes. Don't let it burn! Caramelizing brings out the vegetables' sugars while giving them a pleasant, light brown appearance.

6. Add the beer, sugar, and spices. Lower the flame to simmer the wings for 20 minutes.

7. Remove the wings from their sauce with tongs. Place in a large mixing bowl. Keep warm.

8. Turn off the heat and whisk the butter into the sauce in the skillet until it's smooth and incorporated.

9. Pour the sauce over the wings, making sure they're thoroughly coated.

HOT BULL WINGS

☞ **These** wings are like a red flag to a bull . . . trouble!

3 tablespoons vegetable oil
20 trimmed and separated
  wings
Dash each salt and pepper
½ tablespoon minced
  shallots
½ tablespoon minced fresh
  garlic
¼ cup minced white button
  mushrooms

¼ cup minced prosciutto
⅓ cup Madeira wine
½ cup chicken stock
1 tablespoon chopped fresh
  parsley
2 tablespoons (¼ stick)
  unsalted butter
1 tablespoon hot sauce

1. Heat the oil in a large, heavy skillet over a high flame. Add the wings, sprinkling with salt and pepper, and fry for 8 minutes, or until brown.

2. Add the shallots, garlic, mushrooms, and prosciutto; sauté with the wings until tender and lightly brown, about 4 minutes.

3. Add the Madeira and let the mixture simmer for 4 minutes. Add chicken stock and parsley and simmer for 5 to 8 minutes, or until the sauce starts to thicken.

4. Remove the wings with tongs and place them on a platter. Immediately whisk the butter and hot sauce into the liquid remaining in the skillet until smooth.

5. Pour the sauce over the wings and watch the neighbors pour in!

JOLLY GREEN ONION WINGS

☞ **At** the end of the rainbow is a pot of simmering wings!

2 tablespoons vegetable oil
20 trimmed and separated
  wings
Dash each salt and pepper
1 cup sour cream
1 tablespoon fresh lime juice
½ cup chopped green
  onions (scallions)

1 teaspoon Dijon mustard
1 teaspoon grated fresh
  gingerroot
2 tablespoons chopped fresh
  parsley
½ teaspoon cayenne pepper

1. Heat the oil in a large, heavy skillet over a high flame. Add the wings, sprinkling with salt and pepper, and fry for 10 to 12 minutes, or until golden brown and cooked through. Remove from the heat, set aside, and keep warm.

2. In a large mixing bowl, combine the sour cream, lime juice, green onions, mustard, ginger, parsley, and cayenne. Mix well.

3. Add the wings to the bowl and toss, making sure they're thoroughly coated.

LEMON-BOURBON GLAZED WINGS

☞ **Make** sure you keep the fire department's phone number handy!

⅓ cup sugar	*2 tablespoons (¼ stick)*
1 tablespoon cornstarch	*unsalted butter*
¾ cup cold water	*2 tablespoons vegetable oil*
¾ teaspoon grated lemon	*20 trimmed and separated*
rind	*wings*
1 teaspoon fresh lemon juice	*Dash each salt and pepper*
Dash hot sauce	*⅓ cup bourbon*

1. Whisk the sugar, cornstarch, and cold water in a small saucepan. Bring to a boil over a high flame. Reduce the heat and simmer for 3 minutes.

2. Whisk in the lemon rind, lemon juice, hot sauce, and butter. Turn off the heat and set the mixture aside.

3. In a large, heavy skillet, heat the oil. Add the wings, sprinkling with salt and pepper to seal in their flavor. Fry for 10 to 15 minutes, or until golden brown, firm, and cooked through.

4. Over a high flame, sprinkle the wings with bourbon—then ignite! After 30 seconds, the flames will subside; add the prepared lemon sauce.

5. Transfer the wings to a large mixing bowl and toss, making sure they're thoroughly coated.

LITTLE RED RIDING WINGS

☞ **Little** Red Riding Hood would have been safe if she'd carried these wings in her basket—they'll satisfy any wolf!

3 tablespoons olive oil	*2 garlic cloves, minced*
20 trimmed and separated wings	*1 tablespoon chopped fresh basil*
Dash each salt and pepper	*¼ cup heavy cream*
2 red bell peppers, chopped into ½-inch pieces	*1 tablespoon parmesan cheese*
1 yellow onion, chopped into ½-inch pieces	*Dash hot sauce*
	2 tablespoons unsalted butter

1. Heat the oil in a large, heavy skillet over a high flame. Add the wings, sprinkling with salt and pepper, and fry for 8 minutes, or until brown. Add the peppers, onion, garlic, salt, and pepper. Sauté with the wings until tender and lightly brown, about 4 minutes.

2. Remove the skillet from the heat. With tongs, remove the wings from the pan. Keep the wings warm.

3. Put the cooked vegetables into a food processor and blend until smooth, adding the basil, cheese, hot sauce, and butter. Return the sauce to the skillet, add the wings, and simmer for 3 minutes over a medium flame, stirring to thoroughly coat the wings.

4. Transfer to a platter—and stop believing those fairy tales, for wingness' sake!

MANHATTAN BBQ WINGS

☞ **These** are called Manhattan Wings because so many wing lovers in the Big Apple live in small apartments and can't barbecue. This recipe can be made successfully in a little kitchenette.

½ cup chile sauce
1 tablespoon honey
1 tablespoon soy sauce
½ teaspoon dry mustard
½ teaspoon garlic powder
½ teaspoon cayenne pepper
¼ cup fresh orange juice

2 tablespoons (¼ stick)
*   unsalted butter, melted*
Dash hot sauce
2 tablespoons vegetable oil
20 trimmed and separated
*   wings*
Dash each salt and pepper

1. Mix the chile sauce, honey, soy sauce, mustard, garlic powder, cayenne, orange juice, butter, and hot sauce in a large mixing bowl. Set aside.

2. In a large, heavy skillet, heat the oil over a high flame. Add the wings, sprinkling with salt and pepper to seal in their flavor, and brown them for 8 minutes.

3. Add the prepared sauce, lower the heat, and simmer for 20 minutes. If the sauce becomes too thick, add a little more orange juice to thin it out.

4. Transfer to a large platter. Serve with plenty of napkins!

MICROBREW WINGS

☞ **Every** city has a brewpub, and every brewpub serves wings!

2 tablespoons vegetable oil
20 trimmed and separated
  wings
½ teaspoon garlic powder
½ teaspoon dried thyme
½ teaspoon paprika
½ teaspoon salt
½ teaspoon ground black
  pepper
½ teaspoon caraway seeds

½ cup diced yellow onion
¼ cup diced red onion
6 ounces dark beer
½ tablespoon white vinegar
1 tablespoon light brown
  sugar
1 tablespoon apple juice
¼ cup chicken stock
1 tablespoon unsalted butter

1. Heat the oil in a large, heavy skillet over a high flame. Add the wings and sprinkle with the garlic powder, thyme, paprika, salt, pepper, and caraway seeds. Fry for 8 minutes, or until brown.

2. Add the yellow and red onions. Cook until tender and lightly browned, about 3 minutes.

3. Add the beer to the pan and bring to a low boil. Add vinegar, brown sugar, apple juice, and chicken stock. Continue to simmer over low to medium heat for 8 minutes, or until the wings are cooked through.

4. With tongs, remove the wings from the pan and keep them warm. Continue to simmer the liquid in pan until it thickens. Quickly whisk in the butter until smooth.

5. Return the wings to pan and coat them completely with sauce. Transfer to a platter and serve with a cold microbrew.

NEW YEAR'S WINGS

☞ **Here** is a recipe to cook for your New Year's Eve party. When you make your resolutions, promise to eat more wings than ever.

2 tablespoons vegetable oil
20 trimmed and separated
  wings
Pinch each salt and pepper
½ teaspoon dried thyme

3 tablespoons cognac
2 cups champagne
¾ cup chicken stock
1½ tablespoons tomato paste
1½ cups heavy cream

1. In a large, heavy skillet, heat the oil over a high flame. Add the wings, sprinkling with salt, pepper, and thyme to seal in their flavor. Fry until golden brown, firm, and cooked through, about 8 minutes.

2. Over high heat, splash the wings with cognac and ignite. The flames will subside within about 30 seconds. The pan must be hot.

3. Splash champagne over the wings. Reduce the heat and simmer for 30 seconds.

4. Add the chicken stock and tomato paste, mixing well, and continue to simmer over low heat for 3 minutes.

5. Add the heavy cream. Continue simmering until the sauce is thickened and reduced, leaving the wings slightly coated.

6. Add more salt to the sauce, if needed.

7. Transfer to a large platter and have yourself a happy new year!

ANTISOCIAL WINGS

☞ **This** is a great recipe to rid yourself of unwanted guests. Serve with after-dinner mints!

¼ cup olive oil
1 tablespoon vegetable oil
20 trimmed and separated
   wings
Dash each salt and pepper
1 small onion, diced
1 shallot, diced fine
7 garlic cloves, chopped
½ teaspoon garlic powder

½ teaspoon onion powder
½ teaspoon salt
½ teaspoon ground black
   pepper
½ lemon
2 tablespoons chopped fresh
   parsley
Dash hot sauce

1. In a large, heavy skillet, heat the olive and vegetable oils over a high flame.

2. Add the wings, sprinkling with salt and pepper to seal in their flavor. Fry until the wings are brown and cooked through.

3. Add the onion and shallot. Brown. Add the garlic and cook until lightly browned. Add the garlic and onion powders, and the salt and pepper. Toss everything together. Turn off the heat.

4. Transfer the wings to a large mixing bowl and squeeze lemon juice over them. Add parsley and hot sauce. Toss, making sure the wings are thoroughly coated.

5. Transfer to a large platter and have a "bad breath" day.

"ROSIE" WINGS

☞ I never promised you a rose garden . . . I promised wings. This recipe is dedicated to a fine lady of morning television.

20 wings, trimmed and
*   separated*
2 tablespoons vegetable oil
Dash each salt and pepper
½ cup chopped onion
1 teaspoon (2 cloves)
*   minced garlic*
1 can (12–14 ounces) diced
*   tomatoes, in their juices*

½ cup heavy cream
⅓ cup chopped fresh basil
½ teaspoon salt
½ teaspoon ground black
*   pepper*
½ teaspoon sugar

1. In a large, heavy skillet heat the oil over a high flame. Add the wings, sprinkling with salt and pepper to seal in their flavor while they brown. Fry for 8 minutes, or until brown.

2. Add the onion and garlic and sauté until lightly brown and tender, about 3 minutes.

3. Add the tomatoes and let the mixture simmer over low to medium heat, making sure the wings are thoroughly coated, for 12 minutes, or until the sauce starts to thicken.

4. With tongs, remove the wings from the tomato sauce and set aside; keep warm. Add the cream, basil, salt, pepper, and sugar, and stir until smooth. Return the wings to the now rosy pink sauce, coating them thoroughly.

PRETTY COOL PARSLEY-DILL WINGS

☞ **Reserve** a little of the sauce to dip carrot or celery sticks in.

1 cup mayonnaise
1 cup yogurt
2 teaspoons honey
2 crushed garlic cloves
2 tablespoons Dijon mustard
1 cup chopped fresh parsley
2 tablespoons chopped fresh dill

½ teaspoon fresh lemon juice
2 tablespoons vegetable oil
20 trimmed and separated wings
Pinch each salt and pepper

1. In a large mixing bowl, whisk the mayonnaise, yogurt, honey, garlic, mustard, parsley, dill, and lemon juice until smooth. Set aside.

2. In a large, heavy skillet, heat the oil over a high flame. Add the wings, sprinkling with salt and pepper to seal in their flavor. Fry until brown and cooked through, about 12 minutes.

3. Remove the wings with tongs and place them on paper towels to drain. Transfer them into the mixing bowl with the prepared sauce. Toss, making sure the wings are thoroughly coated. Serve on a large platter with celery and carrot sticks.

SOUTHWESTERN PEANUT WINGS

½ cup chunky peanut butter
½ cup canned unsweetened
   coconut milk
1 dried chipotle pepper
1 teaspoon fresh gingerroot,
   chopped fine
1 tablespoon light brown
   sugar
1 teaspoon soy sauce
1 teaspoon fresh lime juice

¼ teaspoon roasted sesame
   oil
½ teaspoon salt
1 teaspoon onion powder
½ teaspoon turmeric
¼ cup water
¼ cup vegetable oil
20 trimmed and separated
   wings
Dash each salt and pepper

1. In a food processor, combine the peanut butter, coconut milk, chipotle, ginger, and brown sugar. Pulse until smooth.

2. Transfer the puree to a small saucepan. Simmer for 1 minute over a low flame while stirring continuously.

3. Transfer the puree to a large mixing bowl. Whisk in the soy sauce, lime juice, roasted sesame oil, spices, and water.

4. Heat the oil in a large, heavy skillet over a high flame. Add the wings, sprinkling with salt and pepper to seal in their flavor. Fry until brown, crispy, and cooked through, about 12 minutes.

5. Transfer the wings to the sauce bowl with tongs to avoid oil drippings. Toss, making sure the wings are thoroughly coated. Transfer to a large platter.

TERMINATOR CRUNCH WINGS

☞ **Serve** these wings and your friends will "be back!"

1½ cups all-purpose flour
½ teaspoon salt
½ teaspoon ground black
   pepper
½ teaspoon onion powder
½ teaspoon garlic powder

¼ teaspoon cayenne pepper
¼ teaspoon dried thyme
3 cups buttermilk
20 trimmed and separated
   wings
Vegetable oil, for frying

1. In a large mixing bowl, combine the flour, salt, pepper, onion and garlic powders, cayenne, and thyme. Mix well.

2. Pour the buttermilk into a separate, medium bowl.

3. Coat the wings in the seasoned flour, then dip them into the buttermilk. Return the wings to the flour to double-coat them.

4. Heat the oil in a fryer to 350° F. Place the wings in the hot oil and fry for 10 to 12 minutes, or until crunchy, golden brown, and cooked through. Drain on paper towels.

VIRGINIA WINGS

☞ **Everybody** loves crispy fried chicken. This recipe will also go over well with kids, who are not yet capable of withstanding the force of atomic hot sauces.

20 trimmed and separated
  wings
1 cup buttermilk
1 cup all-purpose flour
1 cup cornmeal
1 teaspoon salt
½ teaspoon onion powder

½ teaspoon garlic powder
¼ teaspoon dried thyme
¼ teaspoon ground black
  pepper
Vegetable oil, for deep-
  frying

1. Toss the wings with buttermilk to coat. Marinate for 1 hour in a large plastic bowl in the refrigerator.

2. In a large brown paper bag, shake the flour, cornmeal, salt, onion and garlic powders, thyme, and pepper.

3. Remove the wings from their marinade after 1 hour and place them in the bag with the dry ingredients. Shake until the wings are thoroughly coated.

4. Place the wings on a flat tray in the freezer for 1 hour. This will allow the breading on the wings to solidify before frying. It also eliminates scattered breading in the oil.

5. Heat the oil to 350° F in a fryer, or heat 1 inch of oil in a large, heavy skillet over a high flame.

6. Fry the wings one at a time (to ensure the right oil temperature) for 10 to 15 minutes. Remove each one when it's brown, crispy, and cooked through.

7. Place the wings on paper towels to drain. Transfer to a large platter and serve.

WILD ROASTED-PEPPER WINGS

☞ **The** vegetables in this recipe need to be brushed with vegetable oil and roasted. This can be accomplished by holding them with tongs over an open flame on a gas stove until they're evenly blackened; placing them under a broiler and turning until they're evenly blackened; or grilling them on a barbecue or gas grill. After you've roasted the vegetables, place them in a sealed plastic bag or container while they are still warm to let them "sweat." After about 20 minutes, peel off all the blackened skin and seed the peppers under running water in the sink. You can store any extras in olive oil with a little garlic.

2 tablespoons vegetable oil
20 trimmed and separated
* wings*
Dash each salt and pepper
2 roasted and peeled
* habañero chiles*
2 roasted and peeled
* tomatoes*
2 roasted and peeled red
* bell peppers*

1 roasted and peeled onion
¼ cup chopped fresh
* cilantro*
¼ teaspoon dried oregano
⅛ teaspoon salt
⅛ teaspoon ground black
* pepper*
1 teaspoon fresh lime juice
½ teaspoon hot sauce

1. In a large, heavy skillet, heat the oil over a high flame. Add the wings, sprinkling with salt and pepper. Fry for 10 to 12 minutes, or until brown and cooked through. Remove from the heat and set aside.

2. Place the roasted vegetables in a food processor along with the cilantro, oregano, salt, pepper, lime juice, and hot sauce. Blend until smooth.

3. Pour the vegetable puree into a large mixing bowl and add the wings, tossing to coat.

4. Transfer to a platter, and have a wild wing roast!

YOUR HOT TOMATO WINGS

2 tablespoons vegetable oil
20 trimmed and separated
*   wings*
Dash each salt and pepper
2 cups chopped onion
1 small jalapeño pepper,
*   seeded and minced*
½ tablespoon chile powder

½ teaspoon ground cumin
1 (16-ounce) can whole
*   plum tomatoes,*
*   undrained*
2 tablespoons (¼ stick)
*   unsalted butter*
Dash hot sauce

1. Heat the oil in a large, heavy skillet over a high flame. Add the wings, sprinkling with salt and pepper. Fry for 8 minutes, or until brown.

2. Add the onions, jalapeño, garlic, chile powder, and cumin, and sauté until tender and lightly brown, about 3 minutes.

3. Add the plum tomatoes and juice and simmer over low to medium heat for 20 minutes.

4. With tongs, remove the wings from the tomato sauce and keep warm. Transfer the tomato mixture to a food processor and blend, while adding the butter and hot sauce, until smooth.

5. Return both the wings and the tomato mixture to the skillet and simmer for about 5 minutes over medium heat. The sauce is ready when it easily coats the wings.

GUMBO WINGS

3 tablespoons vegetable oil
20 wings, trimmed and
   separated
4 slices chopped raw bacon
1 cup green bell pepper,
   in ½-inch dice
½ cup celery, in ½-inch dice
½ cup onion, in 1-inch dice
1 pound ground beef or
   ground turkey
1 (28-ounce) can diced
   tomatoes

1 cup chicken stock
¾ teaspoon salt
1 teaspoon dried thyme
½ teaspoon ground allspice
⅛ teaspoon cayenne pepper
⅛ teaspoon ground black
   pepper
1½ cups cooked corn
   (from a can or frozen)
Hot sauce, to taste
   (optional)
6 cups cooked, hot rice

1. In a large, heavy 6-inch-deep pot or pan, heat the oil over a high flame. Brown the wings for 5 to 10 minutes. Add the raw bacon and cook among the wings until it's brown and crispy, about 3 minutes. Remove the wings and bacon with a slotted spoon, reserving the oil and bacon drippings in the pan. Set the wings and bacon aside.

2. In the pot with the drippings, sauté the pepper, celery, and onion until translucent and tender. Add the ground beef or turkey. Brown the meat while stirring it with the vegetables for 5 to 10 minutes over high heat.

3. Return the wings and bacon to the pot. Add the canned tomatoes, chicken stock, salt, thyme, allspice, cayenne, and black pepper and bring to a boil over high heat while stirring. Once the mixture is boiling, lower the heat and simmer the gumbo for 15 minutes.

4. Add the corn. Continue to simmer for 5 minutes. Remove from the heat. Add hot sauce if you like a hotter gumbo.

5. Place a heaping spoon of hot rice on each dinner plate, then pour a heaping ladle of gumbo over it. Make sure you divide the wings equally among everyone. You don't want any fights breaking out at the table, do you?

CHICKEN-WING CHILI

☞ **For** those of you who want it all I have a chicken-wing chili!

2 tablespoons olive oil
2 medium onions, coarsely
    diced
6 garlic cloves, minced
1 pound dried northern
    beans, soaked overnight
    and drained (soaking
    directions can be found
    on the bean package)
1½ quarts chicken stock
2 tablespoons vegetable oil
20 wings, trimmed and
    separated
Dash each salt and pepper
2 fresh jalapeño chiles,
    seeded and minced
1 (6-ounce) can whole green
    chiles, drained, chiles cut
    into small strips

¼ teaspoon ground black
    pepper
2 teaspoons ground cumin
2 teaspoons garlic powder
1 teaspoon ground
    coriander
1 tablespoon granulated
    sugar
1 tablespoon light brown
    sugar
½ teaspoon ground
    allspice
¼ cup chopped fresh
    cilantro
2 cups diced fresh plum
    tomatoes

1. In a large, heavy 6-inch-deep pot or pan, heat the olive oil over high heat. Add the onions and garlic. Brown them for about 5 minutes, then add the soaked beans and chicken stock.

2. Bring the mixture to a boil over high heat. Lower the heat and simmer for 1 to 1½ hours, or until the beans are tender.

3. Remove the pot from the stove. Carefully drain any remaining liquid. Set this liquid and the cooked beans aside.

4. Clean and dry the pot you cooked the beans in. Reheat it over a high flame and add the vegetable oil. When the oil is hot, add the wings; sprinkle with salt and pepper to seal in their flavor while they cook. Brown the wings for 5 to 10 minutes.

5. Add the jalapeño, green chiles, pepper, cumin, garlic powder, coriander, granulated sugar, brown sugar, allspice, cilantro, reserved beans, and 2 cups of bean liquid.

6. Bring to a boil over high heat. Reduce the heat and simmer for 30 minutes, stirring occasionally to prevent the chili from sticking to the bottom of the pot.

7. Stir in the plum tomatoes and turn off the heat. You should be able to stand a spoon up in the chili. If you can't, continue to simmer it until the correct thickness is reached.

8. Serve in bowls topped with sour cream, diced onions, and crackers.

FAST FIRE-DEPARTMENT WINGS

3 tablespoons vegetable oil
20 trimmed and separated
   wings
Dash each salt and pepper
1 large onion, coarsely
   diced
2 garlic cloves, minced
1½ tablespoons chile
   powder
1 teaspoon dried oregano
1 teaspoon ground cumin
1 teaspoon garlic powder
1 teaspoon onion powder

1 (16-ounce) can diced
   tomatoes
1½ cups chicken broth
1 (4-ounce) can chopped
   green chiles
3 fresh jalapeño peppers,
   seeded and chopped fine
⅓ cup fresh cilantro,
   chopped
¼ cup packed light brown
   sugar
Hot sauce, to taste
   (optional)

1. In a large, heavy 6-inch-deep pot or pan, heat the oil over high heat. Add the wings, sprinkling with salt and pepper to seal in their flavor while you brown them for 8 minutes. Add the onion and garlic.

2. Cook until the onion and garlic are translucent and tender. Add the chile powder, oregano, cumin, and garlic and onion powders. Stir until the wings, onion, garlic, and spices are incorporated.

3. Add the diced tomatoes, chicken broth, green chiles, jalapeños, cilantro, and brown sugar.

4. Bring to a boil over high heat. Lower the heat and simmer for 20 minutes. Add hot sauce if more fire-department heat is needed.

WING PAELLA

☞ **Here's** an American version of the classic Spanish dish with the convenience of a one-dish meal . . . Olé!

1 tablespoon virgin olive oil
2 tablespoons vegetable oil
20 trimmed and separated
   wings
Dash each salt and pepper
1 cup chopped onion
3 garlic cloves, minced
1 (16-ounce) can diced
   tomatoes
1½ cups chicken broth
1 small green bell pepper,
   seeded and diced
1 small red bell pepper,
   seeded and diced
½ cup chopped green
   onions (scallions)

2 tablespoons finely
   chopped fresh cilantro
1 teaspoon ground cumin
½ teaspoon saffron threads
½ teaspoon turmeric
½ teaspoon salt
½ teaspoon ground black
   pepper
⅔ cup uncooked long-grain
   rice
1 (16-ounce) can black
   beans, drained and
   rinsed

1. Preheat the oven to 350° F.

2. In a large, heavy 4- to 6-inch-deep pot or authentic paella pan, heat the olive and vegetable oils over high heat. Add the wings. Sprinkle with salt and pepper to seal in their flavor while you brown them.

3. Add the onion and garlic. Lightly brown them along with the wings. Do not burn the garlic; it will taste bitter.

4. Add the tomatoes, chicken broth, green and red peppers, green onions, cilantro, cumin, saffron, turmeric, salt, black pepper, and rice.

5. Stir the ingredients until they're incorporated. Bring to a boil. Reduce the heat and simmer for 3 minutes. Place the pot or paella pan in the oven and bake for 25 to 30 minutes, covered with a lid or aluminum foil. You can also simmer the paella over very low heat for 20 to 25 minutes.

6. Remove the pan from the oven or stove when the rice is tender. Stir in the black beans.

WINGS GO CREOLE

☞ **Want** to protect yourself from Voodoo magic? Stir up a batch of this dish and, before you know it, the spirits of evil will be running!

3 tablespoons vegetable oil
20 trimmed and separated
  wings
Dash each salt and pepper
⅓ cup sweet sherry
½ teaspoon (1 clove)
  minced fresh garlic
½ cup coarsely chopped
  onion
1 cup green bell pepper, in
  ½-inch dice

1 (8-ounce) can stewed
  tomatoes
1½ teaspoons dried basil
1½ teaspoons salt
½ teaspoon garlic powder
½ teaspoon onion powder
1 bay leaf
⅛ teaspoon cayenne pepper
1 teaspoon dried thyme
½ teaspoon hot sauce
6 cups cooked, hot rice

1. In a large, heavy 4- to 6-inch-deep pot, heat the oil over a high flame. Add the wings, sprinkling with salt and pepper to seal in their flavor while you brown them for 5 to 10 minutes.

2. Add the sherry and simmer for 2 minutes. Add the garlic, onion, and peppers and cook until translucent and tender, about 3 minutes.

3. Add the tomatoes, basil, salt, garlic and onion powders, bay leaf, cayenne, thyme, and hot sauce.

4. Bring to a boil over high heat. Reduce the heat and simmer for 5 minutes.

5. Serve over rice.

WINGIN' IT JAMBALAYA

2 tablespoons vegetable oil
20 trimmed and separated
   wings
Dash each salt and pepper
1 tablespoon unsalted butter
½ pound andouille sausage,
   sliced ¼ inch thick (you
   can substitute chorizo
   sausage or diced smoked
   ham)
1 small onion, chopped
3 garlic cloves, sliced into
   thin slivers
½ cup diced celery

1 medium green bell pepper,
   seeded, in ½-inch dice
1 medium red bell pepper,
   seeded, in ½-inch dice
4 diced plum tomatoes
1 cup uncooked long-grain
   rice
½ teaspoon garlic powder
½ teaspoon Cajun seasoning
½ teaspoon ground allspice
1½ cups chicken stock
1 cup dry white wine
Hot sauce, to taste
   (optional)

1. In a large, heavy 6-inch-deep pot or pan, heat the oil over a high flame. Add the wings, sprinkling with salt and pepper to seal in their flavor while you brown them for 5 to 10 minutes. Melt in the butter.

2. Add the sausage, onion, garlic, and celery. Lightly brown for 5 minutes.

3. Add the peppers, tomatoes, rice, garlic powder, Cajun seasoning, and allspice. Stir until the ingredients are incorporated.

4. Pour in the chicken stock and wine. Bring to a boil over high heat, then lower the heat and simmer for 20 minutes, or until the rice is tender. Add hot sauce if you require more heat.

5. Son of a gun, we'll have chicken wings on the Bayou!

ALOHA WINGS

☞ **It** would be nice if, when you arrived in Hawaii, the natives would present you with these wings instead of leis!

¼ cup soy sauce
¼ cup canned crushed
  pineapple
1 tablespoon hoisin *sauce*
½ teaspoon crushed dried
  red pepper
1 tablespoon apple cider
  vinegar
1 tablespoon honey

1 tablespoon light brown
  sugar
1 tablespoon (5 cloves)
  finely chopped fresh
  garlic
½ tablespoon finely chopped
  fresh gingerroot
2 tablespoons dark rum

1. In a large mixing bowl, whisk the soy sauce, crushed pineapple, *hoisin*, crushed pepper, vinegar, honey, brown sugar, garlic, ginger, and rum.

2. Place the wings in the marinade, making sure they are thoroughly coated. Marinate for 4 hours in the refrigerator.

3. Preheat the oven to 375° F. Remove the wings from the marinade with tongs. Reserve the remaining marinade.

4. Place the wings on a 2-inch-deep baking dish, making sure you spread them out flat.

5. Bake for 15 minutes, then turn and baste with the remaining marinade. Bake for an additional 10 to 15 minutes, or until browned and cooked through.

BLUE MONDAY WINGS

☞ **Having** a bad day? Whip up a batch of these wings. The super-crunchy crust will have you up and running in no time.

¼ cup fresh lime juice
¼ cup vegetable oil
½ teaspoon cayenne pepper
2 tablespoons (¼ stick)
   unsalted butter, melted
½ cup blue or yellow
   cornmeal
2 tablespoons all-purpose
   flour

½ teaspoon salt
½ teaspoon ground cumin
¼ teaspoon ground black
   pepper
¼ teaspoon garlic powder
¼ teaspoon onion powder
20 trimmed and separated
   wings

1. Combine the lime juice, vegetable oil, cayenne pepper, and butter in a large mixing bowl. Add the wings and toss to coat. Marinate for 1 hour in the refrigerator.

2. In the meantime, mix the cornmeal, flour, salt, cumin, pepper, and garlic and onion powders in a large brown bag. Shake well to mix the breading thoroughly.

3. Preheat the oven to 350° F. Remove the wings from the marinade with tongs, place them in the bag with the breading, and shake well. Make sure they're thoroughly coated.

4. Remove the wings from the bag one at a time, carefully shaking off any loose coating. Place them on a butter-coated baking sheet; spread them evenly to avoid overcrowding.

5. Bake for 20 to 25 minutes, or until crispy, golden brown, and cooked through. Check every 10 minutes while baking to avoid burning.

CORNY CORN WINGS

☞ **There's** nothing like good old-fashioned American corn. This recipe honors southwestern cooking, in which corn plays an important role.

1 cup cooked corn kernels
1 tablespoon tomato
puree
1 tablespoon honey
1 tablespoon molasses
1 tablespoon fresh lemon
juice
1 tablespoon fresh lime
juice
1 cup vegetable oil

1 teaspoon ground black
pepper
2 jalapeño peppers, seeded
and chopped fine
2 tablespoons chopped fresh
cilantro
1 cup all-purpose flour, for
dusting
20 trimmed and separated
wings

1. Preheat the oven to 350° F.

2. Place the corn, tomato puree, honey, molasses, lemon and lime juices, oil, and black pepper in a food processor. Puree until the mixture resembles a smooth paste. Fold in the jalapeños and cilantro. Mix well. Place in a large mixing bowl.

3. Lightly dust the wings with flour, carefully shaking off any excess. Place wings in the bowl with the pureed mixture. Coat each wing separately by firmly pressing some of the mixture onto it. Place the wings on a buttered baking sheet, spreading them evenly to avoid overcrowding.

4. Bake for 25 to 30 minutes, or until crispy, brown, and cooked through. Check the wings every 10 minutes while baking to avoid burning.

HERB GARDEN WINGS

☞ **This** is a great recipe for anyone who has an herb garden. There is nothing like fresh herbs, so powerful and fragrant. If you don't grow your own, buy some potted herbs at a green market or garden center. Then just keep them on your kitchen windowsill and cut off the required amount.

¼ cup apple juice
½ cup olive oil
2 tablespoons fresh lemon juice
1 tablespoon minced fresh garlic
1 tablespoon chopped fresh basil
1 tablespoon chopped fresh dill
½ teaspoon chopped fresh thyme
½ teaspoon chopped fresh rosemary
½ teaspoon chopped fresh tarragon
½ teaspoon onion powder
½ teaspoon ground black pepper
½ teaspoon salt
20 trimmed and separated wings

1. In a large mixing bowl, combine the apple juice, olive oil, lemon juice, garlic, basil, dill, thyme, rosemary, tarragon, onion powder, pepper, and salt. Add the wings to the marinade and toss, making sure they are thoroughly coated with herbs. Marinate in the refrigerator for 4 hours.

2. Preheat the oven to 350° F. Remove the wings from the marinade with tongs and place on a 2-inch-deep baking dish, spreading them evenly to avoid overcrowding.

3. Bake for 25 to 30 minutes, basting continually, until crispy, brown, and cooked through. Check the wings every 10 minutes while baking.

4. Transfer the wings to a platter and sprinkle with a blend of fresh herbs. Serve with a yogurt- or sour cream–based dip.

HOLLYWOOD GINGER WINGS

2 tablespoons fresh lime juice
2 tablespoons fresh lemon juice
¼ cup teriyaki sauce
3 tablespoons honey
2 tablespoons grated fresh gingerroot

1 tablespoon onion powder
⅛ teaspoon ground cinnamon
⅛ teaspoon salt
¼ cup water
20 trimmed and separated wings

1. In a large mixing bowl, combine the lime and lemon juices, teriyaki sauce, honey, ginger, onion powder, cinnamon, salt, and water. Add the wings to the marinade, tossing to coat. Marinate in the refrigerator for 2 hours.

2. Preheat the oven to 375° F. Remove the wings from the marinade with tongs and place on a 2-inch-deep baking dish, spreading them evenly to avoid overcrowding.

3. Bake for 25 to 30 minutes, basting continually with extra marinade, until crispy, brown, and cooked through. Check the wings every 10 minutes while baking.

GRATEFUL CARAVAN WINGS

☞ **I'm** sure Jerry Garcia would love these if he were still around . . . or do ghosts eat wings, too?

½ cup olive oil
2 tablespoons chopped fresh
  cilantro
2 tablespoons chopped fresh
  parsley
1 small onion, diced
1 tablespoon (5 cloves)
  finely chopped fresh
  garlic

Juice of 1 lemon
Juice of 1 lime
Juice of 1 orange
2 teaspoons ground cumin
3 teaspoons hot sauce
1 teaspoon garlic powder
1 teaspoon onion powder
20 trimmed and separated
  wings

1. In a large mixing bowl, combine the olive oil, cilantro, parsley, onion, garlic, juices, cumin, hot sauce, and garlic and onion powders. Add the wings to the marinade, coating them thoroughly. Marinate in the refrigerator for 2 hours.

2. Preheat the oven to 375° F. Remove the wings from the marinade with tongs and place on a 2-inch-deep baking dish, spreading them evenly.

3. Bake for 25 to 30 minutes, basting continually with extra marinade, until crispy, brown, and cooked through. Check the wings every 10 minutes while baking to avoid burning and sticking.

"MAMA KIN'S" BAKED WINGS

☞ **That** famous rock band from Boston should put these on the menu at their restaurant and throw a "Wing and Smokin' Tea" party!

20 trimmed and separated wings
Pinch each salt and pepper
½ cup cream sherry
¼ cup soy sauce
6 tablespoons water
2 teaspoons light brown sugar
¼ teaspoon crushed dried red pepper

1 garlic clove, chopped fine
½ teaspoon finely chopped fresh gingerroot
2¼ teaspoons cornstarch
½ teaspoon roasted sesame oil
1 tablespoon Dijon mustard
Dash hot sauce

1. Season the wings with salt and pepper. Set aside. In a large mixing bowl, combine the sherry, soy sauce, water, brown sugar, crushed pepper, garlic, and ginger. Add the wings to the bowl and toss to coat evenly. Marinate in the refrigerator for 30 minutes.

2. Preheat the oven to 375° F. Remove the wings from the marinade with tongs and place on a 2-inch-deep baking dish, spreading them evenly. Pour the remaining marinade over the wings.

3. Bake for 25 to 30 minutes, basting continually with extra marinade, until cooked through. Remove the wings from the oven and carefully drain the juices into a small saucepan. Set the pan aside. Keep the wings warm.

4. Blend the cornstarch, sesame oil, mustard, and hot sauce in a small mixing bowl. Whip until smooth.

5. Stir the sauce into the pan with the baking juices. Bring to a boil over a high flame. Lower the heat and simmer and stir the sauce until it's thickened, about 5 minutes.

6. Place the cooked wings on a platter and pour the sauce over them.

MIAMI SPICE WINGS

☞ **Here's** a simple and quick recipe for those who don't want to spend too much time out of the sun.

½ cup plain bread crumbs
4 tablespoons chopped fresh cilantro
2 tablespoons Cajun seasoning
2 garlic cloves, minced

1 teaspoon onion powder
1 cup (½ pound, or 2 sticks) unsalted butter, melted
20 trimmed and separated wings

1. Preheat the oven to 350° F.

2. Mix the bread crumbs, cilantro, Cajun seasoning, garlic, and onion powder in a brown bag, shaking well.

3. Dip the wings one by one into the melted butter, then place them in the brown bag. Shake until the wings are coated with the bread crumb mix.

4. Remove the wings from the bag, carefully shaking off any loose bread crumbs, and spread them evenly on a buttered baking sheet.

5. Bake for 25 to 30 minutes, or until crispy, brown, and cooked through. Check the wings every 10 minutes to avoid burning. If they're browning too fast, lower the oven temperature.

SEASONS OF HELL WINGS

☞ **Make** sure your fire extinguisher is in working order!

½ teaspoon Cajun
   seasoning
2 tablespoons (10 cloves)
   minced fresh garlic
¼ cup soy sauce
2 tablespoons olive oil
½ tablespoon hot sauce
3 tablespoons Dijon mustard
2 tablespoons finely
   chopped green onions
   (scallions)

½ teaspoon salt
¼ teaspoon ground black
   pepper
20 trimmed and separated
   wings
1 cup matzoh meal

1. Preheat the oven to 350° F.

2. Combine the Cajun seasoning, garlic, soy sauce, olive oil, hot sauce, mustard, green onions, salt, and pepper in a large mixing bowl. Add the wings, tossing to coat evenly. Add the matzoh meal and toss it with the wings, making sure that they are evenly coated and that the matzoh meal is absorbed into the liquid. This is a moist breading.

2. Place the wings one by one onto a buttered 1- to 2-inch-deep baking dish, spreading them evenly.

3. Bake for 20 to 25 minutes, or until brown, crispy, and cooked through.

SEEDY AND HOT WINGS

☞ **If** you're feeling low-down and dirty, here's a good one!

½ tablespoon minced fresh garlic
½ cup teriyaki sauce
2 tablespoons light brown sugar
2 tablespoons honey
⅓ cup dry sherry
1 tablespoon apple cider vinegar

1 tablespoon hot sauce
2 tablespoons sesame seeds
2 tablespoons coarsely chopped green onions (scallions)
20 trimmed and separated wings

1. In a large mixing bowl, whisk the garlic, teriyaki sauce, brown sugar, honey, sherry, vinegar, hot sauce, sesame seeds, and green onions.

2. Add the wings to the mixture and marinate for 2 hours in the refrigerator.

3. Preheat the oven to 375° F. Remove the wings from the marinade with tongs and spread evenly on a buttered 2-inch-deep baking dish.

4. Bake for 25 to 30 minutes, occasionally basting and turning, until brown and cooked through. Transfer to a platter and serve.

SUNSHINE STATE WINGS

☞ **This** refreshing recipe will put you in a good mood on a rainy day wherever you are.

½ cup teriyaki sauce
Juice of 3 oranges
1 tablespoon light brown
   sugar
1 tablespoon honey
1 small red onion, diced
1 tablespoon fresh lime
   juice
½ tablespoon grated lime
   peel

1 teaspoon onion powder
½ teaspoon dried ginger
½ teaspoon prepared
   mustard
½ teaspoon turmeric
1 teaspoon hot sauce
20 trimmed and separated
   wings

1. In a large mixing bowl, whisk the teriyaki, orange juice, brown sugar, honey, red onion, lime juice and rind, onion powder, ginger, mustard, turmeric, and hot sauce.

2. Add the wings to the mixture and marinate for 2 hours in the refrigerator.

3. Preheat the oven to 375° F. Remove the wings from the marinade with tongs and spread evenly on a 2-inch-deep buttered baking dish.

4. Bake for 25 to 30 minutes, occasionally basting and turning, until brown and cooked through. Transfer to a platter and serve.

SUN-DRIED TOMATO WINGS

☞ **This** recipe proves that sun-dried tomatoes are useful for more than pasta dishes and salads.

½ cup soaked sun-dried tomatoes, drained (to soak, pour enough boiling water over them to cover and let them stand for 10 minutes)
2 garlic cloves
⅛ teaspoon cayenne pepper
⅛ teaspoon onion powder
⅛ teaspoon salt

⅛ teaspoon ground black pepper
1 teaspoon chopped fresh basil
1 cup mayonnaise
20 trimmed and separated wings
¼ cup olive oil
Dash each salt and pepper

1. In a food processor, blend the tomatoes, garlic, and spices until they're chopped fine. Add the mayonnaise and continue blending until a smooth paste forms. Transfer to a large mixing bowl with a rubber spatula. Set aside.

2. Preheat the oven to 375° F. Spread the wings evenly on a buttered 1- to 2-inch-deep baking dish. Brush them with olive oil and sprinkle with salt and pepper.

3. Bake for 25 to 30 minutes, or until crispy, brown, and cooked through. Remove from the oven and drain off excess oil. Let the wings cool for 5 minutes.

4. Toss the wings in the bowl with the sun-dried tomato mixture, coating them thoroughly.

TABASCO-ONION WINGS

☞ I love fried onions on top of steak, chops, and mashed potatoes. Here's a way to eat fried onions with wings. Serve them with blue cheese or ranch dip.

1/3 cup mayonnaise
1/8 teaspoon onion powder
1/8 teaspoon garlic powder
1/8 teaspoon dried basil
1/8 teaspoon dried thyme
1/4 cup Tabasco sauce

1 (12-ounce) can Durkee's
  french-fried onions,
  crumbled
3/4 cup crushed cornflakes
20 trimmed and separated
  wings

1. Preheat the oven to 325° F.

2. In a large mixing bowl, combine the mayonnaise, onion and garlic powders, basil, thyme, and Tabasco until smooth. Set aside.

3. Combine the fried onions and cornflakes in a large bowl. Mix well.

4. Dip the wings one at a time into the mayonnaise mix, then press into the onion-and-cornflake mix. Roll them through the breading to coat them completely.

5. Spread the wings evenly on a buttered baking sheet.

6. Bake for 20 to 25 minutes, or until crispy, brown, and cooked through. Check the wings every 5 minutes; if the crust is browning too fast, cover the wings with aluminum foil.

WANG TANGO WINGS

☞ **These** wings will put you in a spin once you try them.

⅓ cup vegetable oil
2 small onions, minced
2 garlic cloves, minced
2 tablespoons honey
1 tablespoon light brown
   sugar
6 tablespoons ketchup
2 tablespoons tomato paste
4 teaspoons Worcestershire
   sauce

1 teaspoon crushed dried
   red pepper flakes
1 tablespoon black raisins
1 teaspoon ground allspice
½ teaspoon onion powder
20 trimmed and separated
   wings

1. Preheat the oven to 375° F.

2. Heat the oil in a small saucepan over a high flame. Add the onions and garlic; sauté until lightly browned, about 3 minutes.

3. Add the honey, brown sugar, ketchup, and tomato paste. Reduce the heat and simmer while adding the Worcestershire, red pepper flakes, raisins, allspice, and onion powder. Simmer for 3 minutes over a low flame.

4. Turn off the heat and carefully pour the mixture into a blender or food processor. Puree until it's smooth, then pour into a large mixing bowl. Let the mixture cool for 5 minutes.

5. Add the wings to the mixture, coating them thoroughly.

6. Spread the wings evenly on a buttered 2-inch-deep baking dish.

7. Bake for 25 to 30 minutes, or until brown and cooked through. Transfer to a platter and put on your dancing shoes!

WHERE'S MY JOHN WAYNE WINGS

☞ **Eat** these wings and ride off into the sunset . . .

½ cup vegetable oil
20 trimmed and separated
   wings
Pinch each salt and pepper
1 large onion, chopped fine
2 garlic cloves, minced
1½ cups ketchup
¼ cup packed light brown
   sugar
2 tablespoons apple cider
   vinegar

1 teaspoon Worcestershire
   sauce
1 teaspoon prepared
   mustard
½ teaspoon chile powder
½ teaspoon onion powder
½ teaspoon garlic powder
2 jalapeño chiles, minced
   fine

1. Preheat the oven to 375° F.

2. Heat the oil in a large skillet over high heat. Carefully add the wings to the skillet, sprinkling with salt and pepper to seal in their flavor while you brown them. After 10 minutes, remove the wings from the pan with tongs. Reserve the drippings in the pan.

2. Add the onion and garlic to the pan and place over high heat to brown—about 3 minutes. Stir in the ketchup, brown sugar, vinegar, Worcestershire, mustard, spices, and jalapeños. Bring to a boil, then reduce the heat and simmer for 10 minutes. Remove the sauce from the heat and transfer to a large mixing bowl.

3. Add the wings to the sauce, coating them thoroughly.

4. Spread the wings evenly on a buttered 2-inch-deep baking dish. Bake for 10 to 15 minutes, or until brown and glazed.

VERMONT WINTER WINGS

☞ **Think** of Vermont and you're likely to think of cozy, snowy winter nights. These wings are perfect for a gathering around the fire.

2 tablespoons (¼ stick)
    unsalted butter
½ Red Delicious apple,
    cored, peeled, and diced
    fine
1 small onion, diced fine
½ cup ketchup
1 cup apple cider
¼ cup prepared mustard
½ cup real maple syrup
2 tablespoons apple cider
    vinegar

1 teaspoon hot sauce
1 teaspoon ground black
    pepper
1 teaspoon salt
½ teaspoon ground
    cinnamon
½ teaspoon onion powder
20 trimmed and separated
    wings

1. In a small saucepan, melt the butter over a medium flame. Add the apple and diced onion and sauté until tender. Add the ketchup, cider, mustard, syrup, vinegar, hot sauce, pepper, salt, cinnamon, and onion powder. Simmer for 2 minutes.

2. Remove the marinade from the heat and pour it into a large mixing bowl. Cool for 20 minutes.

3. Add the wings to the cooled marinade, coating them thoroughly. Marinate in the refrigerator for 2 hours.

4. Preheat the oven to 375° F. Remove the wings from the marinade with tongs and spread evenly on a buttered baking sheet.

5. Bake for 25 to 30 minutes, or until brown, glazed, and cooked through. Transfer to a platter.

6. Put on your skis and drink a glass of spiced cider.

ANCHO FIRE WINGS

☞ **Ancho** chiles can be bought at most supermarkets or by mail order. To soften dried chiles, place them in a bowl with hot water and let them soak for two hours.

10 dried ancho chiles
(remove seeds and stems)
1 garlic clove
½ teaspoon salt
2 tablespoons tequila
2 tablespoons fresh lime
juice
½ cup olive oil
1 tablespoon chopped fresh
cilantro
20 trimmed and separated
wings

1. In a food processor, puree the chiles, garlic, salt, tequila, lime juice, olive oil, and cilantro. Transfer to a large mixing bowl. Add the wings, coating them thoroughly.

2. Marinate the wings for 4 hours in the refrigerator.

3. Remove the wings from the marinade and place on a low- to medium-heat grill. Baste, turn, and cook for 25 minutes, or until glazed, firm, and cooked through.

4. Transfer to a platter and serve with a cool sauce, like blue cheese or ranch.

BARREL WINGS

☞ **This** sauce is called Barrel thanks to the unique flavor of Jack Daniels whiskey, which is aged in oaken barrels. This sauce also works well with pork and beef.

2 tablespoons vegetable oil
¼ cup chopped onion
¼ cup chopped red onion
1 garlic clove, minced
*¼ cup diced green onions
   (scallions)*
¼ cup Jack Daniels whiskey
2 cups ketchup
¼ cup apple cider vinegar
¼ cup Worcestershire sauce
1 tablespoon molasses
*2 tablespoons light brown
   sugar*

*2 tablespoons prepared
   mustard*
2 tablespoons soy sauce
1 tablespoon Tabasco sauce
*½ teaspoon ground black
   pepper*
½ teaspoon cayenne pepper
*¼ cup (½ stick) unsalted
   butter*
*20 trimmed and separated
   wings*

1. In a large saucepan, heat the oil over a high flame. Add the onion, red onion, garlic, and green onions. Sauté until golden brown and tender. Add the Jack Daniels and simmer for 3 minutes over a reduced flame.

2. Add the ketchup, vinegar, Worcestershire, molasses, mustard, soy sauce, Tabasco, pepper, and cayenne. Bring to a boil over a high flame, then reduce the heat and simmer for 20 minutes. Remove from the heat.

3. Vigorously whisk the butter into the sauce until smooth. Set aside.

4. Place the wings on a low- to medium-heat grill or barbecue. Generously brush them with the Barrel Sauce. Baste and turn, then brush again. Cook the wings for 25 to 30 minutes, or until glazed and cooked through. Transfer to a platter and enjoy.

BEER BOY PAULINO WINGS

☞ **Beer** Boy Paulino is one of the best broiler cooks I've ever seen. To relieve the tension of his demanding job at busy Skippers Pub in Northport, New York, he likes to drink beer—about a case a night! How he does it, nobody knows. Does he get intoxicated? No, not really. He's just a human beer machine—and a great guy!

¼ cup barbecue sauce
½ cup beer (of your choice)
20 trimmed and separated
  wings

½ teaspoon hot sauce
2 tablespoons (¼ stick)
  unsalted butter

1. First, grab a cold beer for yourself.

2. Then heat the barbecue sauce, beer, and hot sauce in a small saucepan over a high flame. Once the mixture is boiling, reduce the heat and simmer for 3 minutes. Remove from the heat. Whisk in the butter until smooth, and set aside.

3. Place the wings on a grill at low heat. Brush generously with the sauce and cook, frequently basting and turning, for 25 to 30 minutes, or until glazed and cooked through.

4. Transfer to a platter, crack another cold one, and have some potato salad, too!

BLUE RIBBON CHEESY WINGS

☞ **It** is customary to serve wings with blue cheese dressing on the side. How about a recipe with blue cheese *on* the wings?

2 tablespoons vegetable oil
1 tablespoon white vinegar
1 teaspoon hot sauce
Dash each salt and pepper
20 trimmed and separated
   wings
1 cup yogurt

2 tablespoons crumbled blue
   cheese
2 tablespoons mayonnaise
½ teaspoon celery salt
¼ teaspoon ground black
   pepper

1. In a large mixing bowl, whisk the oil, vinegar, and hot sauce. Sprinkle salt and pepper on the wings and add them to the bowl, coating them thoroughly. Let the wings marinate for 2 hours in the refrigerator.

2. Meanwhile, make the sauce. In a large bowl, whisk the yogurt, blue cheese, mayonnaise, celery salt, and black pepper together until smooth. Set aside.

3. Remove the wings from the marinade with tongs and place on a low- to medium-heat grill. Cook for 20 to 25 minutes, frequently basting and turning, until golden brown and cooked through.

BRUSHFIRE WINGS

☞ **Be** careful when preparing these wings outside—I didn't call them brushfire for nothing!

1 tablespoon vegetable oil
½ cup diced green bell
* pepper*
½ cup diced onion
1 garlic clove, minced
½ cup Frank's Red Hot
* Sauce*
½ cup ginger ale

2 tablespoons honey
1 tablespoon light brown
* sugar*
20 trimmed and separated
* wings*
1 tablespoon vegetable oil
Dash each salt and pepper
⅛ teaspoon cayenne pepper

1. In a medium saucepan, heat the oil over a high flame. Add the green pepper, onion, and garlic and sauté until lightly browned. Add the hot sauce, ginger ale, honey, and brown sugar.

2. Reduce the heat and simmer the sauce for 8 to 10 minutes, or until it's thick enough to stick to a basting brush. Remove from the heat and set aside.

3. Place the wings in a large mixing bowl. Sprinkle the oil, salt, pepper, and cayenne over them and mix well, making sure they're coated and seasoned.

4. Remove the wings from the bowl and place on a low- to medium-heat grill or barbecue. Brush the wings with the prepared basting sauce while turning them frequently. Cook for 25 to 30 minutes, or until glazed and cooked through.

5. Transfer to a serving platter and have a few water buckets handy, just in case.

BULL RIDER RODEO WINGS

☞ **At** the rodeo, you might get more attention from the riders if you toss them these wings instead of roses!

½ cup virgin olive oil
½ cup fresh orange juice
¼ cup cream sherry
1 teaspoon orange zest (use a zester)
1 tablespoon fresh lemon juice
1 tablespoon fresh lime juice

3 garlic cloves, minced
2 teaspoons salt
¼ teaspoon cayenne pepper
¼ teaspoon hot sauce
1 teaspoon honey
20 trimmed and separated wings

1. In a large mixing bowl, whisk the oil, orange juice, sherry, orange zest, lemon and lime juices, garlic, salt, cayenne, hot sauce, and honey. Add the wings, coating them thoroughly. Marinate for 4 hours in the refrigerator.

2. Remove the wings from the marinade with tongs. Place on a low- to medium-heat grill for 25 to 30 minutes, frequently turning and basting, until golden brown and cooked through.

3. Transfer to a platter and ride the rodeo!

CAROLINA ON MY MIND WINGS

☞ **There's** more on my mind than Carolina when I'm eating these wings.

¼ cup red wine vinegar
¼ cup apple cider vinegar
1 teaspoon Dijon mustard
1 tablespoon prepared
*   yellow mustard*
2 teaspoons honey
1 teaspoon maple syrup
2 teaspoons Worcestershire
*   sauce*
½ teaspoon hot sauce
⅓ cup vegetable oil

1 tablespoon finely chopped
*   fresh rosemary*
1 tablespoon finely chopped
*   fresh thyme*
1 teaspoon finely chopped
*   shallots*
2 teaspoons finely chopped
*   red onion*
20 trimmed and separated
*   wings*

1. In a large mixing bowl, combine the vinegars, Dijon mustard, prepared mustard, honey, maple syrup, Worcestershire, hot sauce, vegetable oil, rosemary, thyme, shallots, and red onion.

2. Add the wings, coating them thoroughly. Marinate for 5 hours in the refrigerator.

3. Remove the wings from marinade with tongs. Place on a low- to medium-heat grill for 25 to 30 minutes, frequently turning and basting, until golden brown and cooked through.

4. Transfer to a platter and enjoy this peculiar recipe.

COFFEEHOUSE WINGS

☞ **I** must dedicate this recipe to the coffeehouses across the country. They are an oasis for the weary author or anyone who needs a recharge. Another refill please . . .

½ cup ketchup
⅓ cup strong black coffee
1 tablespoon light brown
  sugar
1 tablespoon apple cider
  vinegar
2 teaspoons Worcestershire
  sauce

2 teaspoons vegetable oil
⅛ teaspoon cayenne pepper
20 trimmed and separated
  wings
2 tablespoons vegetable oil
Dash each salt and pepper

1. In a small saucepan over a high flame, mix the ketchup, coffee, brown sugar, vinegar, Worcestershire, oil, and cayenne. Bring to a boil while stirring, then reduce the heat and simmer for 8 minutes. Once the mixture is thick enough to stick to a basting brush, remove it from the heat and set aside.

2. In a large mixing bowl, combine the wings with the oil, salt, and pepper, coating them thoroughly.

3. Remove the wings from the bowl with tongs. Place on a low- to medium-heat grill or barbecue and brush generously with sauce. Turn and baste the wings for 25 to 30 minutes, or until glazed and cooked through.

4. Transfer to a platter and treat yourself to a cup of java.

CHILLY WILLY WINGS

☞ **Chilly** Willy is a neighborhood friend who hangs around our house, hoping to sample some wings. This recipe was developed for him. Willy can sometimes be found sleeping in a lawn chair with a pan of the lasagna or baked ziti his mother likes to make for us. "You have to eat more than wings—mangia, mangia," she says. Thanks for the advice, mom . . . we do love your pasta.

¼ cup minced fresh ginger root
¼ cup soy sauce
¼ cup sweet sherry
2 tablespoons fresh lime juice
2 tablespoons fresh orange juice
1 tablespoon light brown sugar

½ cup vegetable oil
1 teaspoon crushed dried red pepper
2 tablespoons chopped fresh cilantro
1 tablespoon chopped green onions (scallions)
20 trimmed and separated wings

1. In a large mixing bowl, whisk the ginger, soy sauce, sherry, lime and orange juices, brown sugar, oil, crushed pepper, cilantro, and green onions.

2. Add the wings to the marinade, coating them thoroughly. Marinate for 5 hours in the refrigerator.

3. Remove the wings from the marinade with tongs and place on a low- to medium-heat grill. Baste and turn the wings until they're brown, glazed, and cooked through, about 25 to 30 minutes. Transfer to a platter.

DOWN-HOME WINGS

3 tablespoons yellow
  mustard
3 tablespoons mayonnaise
½ cup diced green onions
  (scallions)
½ teaspoon dried or fresh
  thyme
½ teaspoon dried or fresh
  dill

2 garlic cloves, minced
½ teaspoon cayenne pepper
¼ teaspoon ground black
  pepper
½ teaspoon onion powder
20 trimmed and separated
  wings

1. In a large mixing bowl, combine the mustard, mayonnaise, green onions, thyme, dill, garlic, cayenne, black pepper, and onion powder. Mix well.

2. Place the wings on a low- to medium-heat grill or barbecue. Brush generously with the basting mixture. Continue to baste and turn the wings for 25 to 30 minutes, or until brown and cooked through.

3. Transfer to a platter.

GINGER MEETS ABBY WINGS

☞ **They** met each other over a plate of wings . . .

½ cup apricot preserves

2 tablespoons fresh lemon juice

2 tablespoons fresh orange juice

1 tablespoon minced fresh gingerroot

2 teaspoons Dijon mustard

½ teaspoon salt

½ teaspoon ground black pepper

1 teaspoon chopped fresh mint

20 trimmed and separated wings

1. In a small saucepan, mix the preserves, lemon and orange juices, ginger, mustard, salt, pepper, and mint. Bring to a boil over a high flame, then reduce the heat and simmer for 3 minutes, or until the sauce is smooth and dissolved. Remove from the heat and set aside.

2. Place the wings on a low- to medium-heat grill or barbecue. Brush generously with the basting sauce. Continue to baste and turn the wings for 25 to 30 minutes, or until glazed and cooked through. Transfer to a platter.

GRILLED MINT CHICKEN WINGS

☞ **Chicken** wings as a breath freshener?

1 cup nonfat yogurt

2 garlic cloves, minced

¼ cup chopped fresh mint

½ teaspoon ground cumin

¼ teaspoon chile powder

¼ teaspoon sugar

¼ teaspoon salt

¼ teaspoon ground black pepper

¼ teaspoon onion powder

¼ teaspoon cayenne pepper

20 trimmed and separated wings

1. In a large mixing bowl, whisk the yogurt, garlic, mint, cumin, chile powder, sugar, salt, pepper, onion powder, and cayenne until smooth.

2. Add the wings to the marinade, coating them thoroughly. Marinate in the refrigerator for 4 hours.

3. Remove the wings from the marinade with tongs and place on a low- to medium-heat grill. Baste and turn the wings frequently for 25 to 30 minutes, or until brown and cooked through.

4. Transfer the wings to a platter. No mouthwash required after these!

GRILLED SUMMERTIME WINGS

½ cup fresh lemon juice
⅓ cup olive oil
½ teaspoon fresh lime juice
2 tablespoons chopped fresh
* mint*
½ teaspoon paprika

½ teaspoon ground cumin
¼ teaspoon salt
¼ teaspoon ground black
* pepper*
20 trimmed and separated
* wings*

1. In a large mixing bowl, whisk the lemon juice, olive oil, lime juice, mint, paprika, cumin, salt, and pepper until smooth.

2. Add the wings to the marinade, coating them thoroughly. Marinate in the refrigerator for 4 hours.

3. Remove the wings from the marinade with tongs and place on a low- to medium-heat grill or barbecue. Turn and baste for 25 to 30 minutes, or until brown and cooked through.

"HONEY, I MUST GRILL WINGS"

☞ **Here's** an escape from taking out the garbage!

1 tablespoon mayonnaise
1 tablespoon Dijon mustard
⅓ cup packed light brown
   sugar
1 tablespoon soy sauce
2 tablespoons honey

½ teaspoon crushed dried
   red pepper
1 teaspoon finely diced
   green onions (scallions)
20 trimmed and separated
   wings

1. In a large mixing bowl, combine the mayonnaise, mustard, brown sugar, soy sauce, honey, crushed pepper, and green onions. Mix until smooth.

2. Place the wings on a low- to medium-heat grill. Brush generously with the basting mixture, and continue to baste and turn the wings for 25 to 30 minutes, or until brown and cooked through.

3. Transfer to a platter. Receive raves from your companion, who might well relieve you of garbage duty!

HOT ROD WINGS

☞ **The** name speaks for itself. Do you think Mr. Rodman would like these wings?

2 tablespoons olive oil
⅓ cup fresh lemon juice
1 teaspoon fresh lime juice
1 tablespoon finely chopped
   jalapeño pepper

1 dried, smoked chipotle
   pepper, crushed
1 tablespoon chicken stock
1 teaspoon minced fresh
   gingerroot

> 2 teaspoons minced fresh
>   garlic
> 2 teaspoons dried thyme
> Dash hot sauce

> ½ teaspoon garlic powder
> ½ teaspoon onion powder
> 20 trimmed and separated
>   wings

1. In a large mixing bowl, whisk the oil, lemon and lime juices, jalapeño, chipotle, chicken stock, ginger, garlic, thyme, hot sauce, and garlic and onion powders until smooth.

2. Add the wings to the bowl and marinate in the refrigerator for 4 hours.

3. Remove the wings from the marinade with tongs and place on a low- to medium-heat grill. Baste and turn for 25 to 30 minutes, or until the wings are brown and cooked through. Transfer to a platter and watch the basketball game with the wings dedicated to you-know-who.

JOHNNY APPLESEED WINGS

☞ **Johnny** Appleseed was a drifter in America's early days who walked from town to town teaching people to grow apple trees. This recipe would surely make him proud. Maybe I should travel the country barefoot and teach people to prepare wings!

> 1 cup apple cider
> ⅓ cup apple cider vinegar
> ⅓ cup chopped green
>   onions (scallions)
> ¼ cup vegetable oil
> 2 tablespoons honey
> 1 tablespoon light brown
>   sugar

> 2 tablespoons A-1 sauce
> 1½ teaspoons chopped fresh
>   mint
> 1 teaspoon salt
> ¼ teaspoon ground black
>   pepper
> 20 trimmed and separated
>   wings

1. In a small saucepan, whisk the cider, vinegar, green onions, oil, honey, brown sugar, A-1 sauce, mint, salt, and pepper until smooth. Bring to a boil over a high flame, then reduce the heat and simmer for 10 minutes. Remove from the heat, transfer to a large mixing bowl, and let the marinade cool for 20 minutes.

2. Place the wings in the cooled marinade and marinate for 5 hours in the refrigerator.

3. Remove the wings from the marinade with tongs and place on a low- to medium-heat grill. Baste and turn the wings frequently for 25 to 30 minutes, or until brown and cooked through.

4. Transfer to a platter and remember, a Johnny Appleseed wing a day keeps the doctor away!

LUCIFER STICKS

☞ **One** night I awoke in a sweat after a hellish nightmare, only to find this recipe from somebody with a pitchfork left behind on my night table.

⅓ cup fresh lemon juice
½ tablespoon crushed dried red pepper
½ tablespoon salt
½ teaspoon cayenne pepper
½ tablespoon coarse-cracked black pepper

2 garlic cloves, minced
⅓ cup virgin olive oil
Dash or more hot sauce
20 trimmed and separated wings

1. In a large mixing bowl, combine the lemon juice, crushed pepper, salt, cayenne, pepper, garlic, oil, and hot sauce.

2. Add the wings to the marinade, coating them thoroughly. Marinate for 24 hours in the refrigerator.

3. Remove the wings from the marinade with tongs and place on a low- to medium-heat grill or barbecue. Baste and turn for 25 to 30 minutes, or until brown and cooked through.

4. Transfer to a platter and have ice water handy!

MAINE GLAZED WINGS

1 cup cranberry sauce (use
   the kind with the whole
   cranberries, not the jelly
   kind that comes in cans)
½ cup raspberry jam
¼ cup apple cider vinegar
½ tablespoon light brown
   sugar

1 fresh jalapeño pepper,
   seeded and minced
¼ teaspoon cayenne
   pepper
¼ teaspoon salt
20 trimmed and separated
   wings

1. In a food processor, combine the cranberry sauce, jam, vinegar, brown sugar, jalapeño, cayenne, and salt. Blend until pureed.

2. Place the wings on a low- to medium-heat grill or barbecue. Brush generously with the basting mixture. Baste and turn the wings frequently for 25 to 30 minutes, or until glazed and cooked through. Transfer to a platter.

QUICK BILLY'S CHILE WINGS

☞ **If** you're in a hurry, don't worry—try these!

½ cup bottled chile sauce

¼ cup barbecue sauce (I like
    Bull's-Eye brand)

2 tablespoons finely
    chopped fresh cilantro

½ teaspoon hot sauce

½ teaspoon onion powder

½ teaspoon garlic powder

20 trimmed and separated
    wings

1. In a large mixing bowl, combine the chile sauce, barbecue sauce, cilantro, hot sauce, and onion and garlic powders. Mix until smooth.

2. Place the wings on a low- to medium-heat grill or barbecue, brushing generously with the basting sauce. Baste and turn the wings frequently until glazed and cooked through, about 25 to 30 minutes.

3. Transfer to a lunch box and eat them on the go!

RASPBERRY BERET WINGS

☞ **"She** wore a raspberry beret, the kind you find in a hot-sauce store."

⅓ cup raspberry vinegar

3 tablespoons molasses

¼ cup Dijon mustard

2 teaspoons Tabasco sauce

2 teaspoons Worcestershire
    sauce

2 tablespoons brandy

⅓ cup vegetable oil

4 garlic cloves, minced

1 teaspoon dried oregano

½ teaspoon dried thyme

½ teaspoon onion powder

20 trimmed and separated
    wings

1. In a large mixing bowl, combine the vinegar, molasses, mustard, Tabasco, Worcestershire, brandy, oil, garlic, oregano, thyme, and onion powder; mix well.

2. Add the wings to the marinade, coating them thoroughly. Marinate, refrigerated, for 4 hours.

3. Remove the wings from the marinade with tongs and place on a low- to medium-heat grill. Baste and turn for 25 to 30 minutes, or until glazed, brown, and cooked through. Transfer to a platter.

RUB-A-DUB-DUB WINGS

☞ **No,** you don't have to rub the genie's lamp; just try this spice rub to flavor grilled or baked wings.

*20 trimmed and separated
  wings
2 tablespoons olive oil
2 teaspoons sugar
1 teaspoon ground
  cinnamon
1 teaspoon ground
  coriander*

*1 teaspoon ground cumin
1 teaspoon ground
  cardamom
½ teaspoon salt
½ teaspoon ground black
  pepper
⅛ teaspoon cayenne
  pepper*

1. In a large mixing bowl, combine the wings with the olive oil, coating them thoroughly. Set aside.

2. Place all the dry ingredients in a medium plastic bowl with a lid. Cover the bowl and shake until the spices are well mixed.

3. Add the spice mixture to the wings, tossing to coat well; make sure the spices are evenly distributed over the wings. Place the wings in the refrigerator for 1 hour to develop the rub's flavor.

4. Place the wings on a low- to medium-heat grill or barbecue for 25 to 30 minutes, turning frequently, until brown and cooked through. You can also bake these wings by placing them on a buttered baking sheet with a 1-inch rim. Bake in a 350° F oven for 25 to 30 minutes, or until brown and cooked through. Transfer to a platter.

RUMMY DUMMY WINGS

☞ I found this recipe inside a bottle that had washed ashore, signed by no less than Captain Blackbeard!

¼ cup soy sauce
2 tablespoons dark rum
⅓ cup finely minced onion
½ tablespoon finely minced fresh gingerroot
1 garlic clove, finely minced
3 tablespoons unsalted butter, melted

3 tablespoons ketchup
½ teaspoon sugar
½ cup red wine (a Merlot works well)
⅛ teaspoon ground black pepper
20 trimmed and separated wings

1. In a large mixing bowl, combine the soy sauce, rum, onion, ginger, garlic, butter, ketchup, sugar, wine, and pepper. Mix well.

2. Add the wings to the marinade, coating them thoroughly. Marinate in the refrigerator for 4 hours.

3. Remove the wings from the marinade with tongs and place on a low- to medium-heat grill, basting and turning frequently, for 25 to 30 minutes, or until brown and cooked through.

4. Transfer to a platter and pull out your treasure map. Happy gold hunting!

SUNBURNED WINGS

☞ **These** are "sunburned" because these wings have a deep, beautiful color after they've been grilled.

½ cup Dijon mustard

2 tablespoons fresh orange juice

2 tablespoons canned pineapple juice

1 teaspoon fresh orange zest (use a zester)

1 teaspoon lemon zest (use a zester)

1 tablespoon vegetable oil

½ tablespoon fresh lemon juice

½ teaspoon sugar

¼ teaspoon ground black pepper

¼ teaspoon crushed dried red pepper

20 trimmed and separated wings

1. In a large mixing bowl, combine the mustard, orange and pineapple juices, orange and lemon zests, oil, lemon juice, sugar, black pepper, and crushed red pepper. Mix well.

2. Add the wings to the marinade, coating them thoroughly. Marinate in the refrigerator for 4 hours.

3. Remove the wings from the marinade with tongs and place on a low- to medium-heat grill, basting and turning frequently, for 25 to 30 minutes, or until brown and cooked through.

4. Transfer to a platter and pull out your tanning lotion.

INTERNATIONAL WING RECIPES

Now that you've sampled some wing recipes from across America, it's time to try some international wings. Although the use of chicken wings is popular in international cooking, "wing-mania" has not reached the proportions abroad that it has in the United States. I guess it's time for a worldwide wing revolution!

These wing recipes make use of ingredients that can be found in neighborhood ethnic shops across the country.

BANGKOK ON FIRE WINGS

☞ **Thai** cooking is hot! If you haven't tried this cuisine, visit a local Thai restaurant; chances are there's one near you. Most ingredients, like fish sauce, are readily available in supermarkets. If not, try mail order or an Asian market.

1/2 (12-ounce) can unsweetened coconut milk
1 teaspoon hot sauce
1 1/2 tablespoons fish sauce (nam pla)
1 1/2 tablespoons rice wine vinegar
1/2 tablespoon fresh lime juice
1/2 tablespoon soy sauce
1 teaspoon light brown sugar
1/2 tablespoon curry powder
2 garlic cloves, minced
1/2 teaspoon crushed dried red pepper
20 trimmed and separated wings

1. In a large mixing bowl, combine the coconut milk, hot sauce, fish sauce, vinegar, lime juice, soy sauce, brown sugar, curry, garlic, and crushed pepper. Mix well.

2. Add the wings to the marinade, coating them thoroughly. Place the bowl with the wings in the refrigerator for 24 hours in order to develop full flavor.

3. Remove the wings from the marinade with tongs and place on a low- to medium-heat grill. Baste and turn frequently for 25 to 30 minutes, or until brown and cooked through. Transfer to a platter.

BORDER PATROL WINGS

☞ **Don't** let them catch you smuggling these wings over the border! You might end up cooking for the guards for the rest of your life.

¼ cup vegetable oil
¼ cup olive oil
1 teaspoon fresh lemon juice
1 teaspoon fresh lime juice
1 teaspoon light brown sugar
½ teaspoon chile powder
½ teaspoon paprika
1 teaspoon crushed dried red pepper
½ teaspoon hot sauce
½ teaspoon onion powder
½ teaspoon garlic powder
1 tablespoon chopped fresh cilantro
½ teaspoon salt
½ teaspoon ground black pepper
20 trimmed and separated wings

1. In a large mixing bowl, combine the vegetable and olive oils, lemon and lime juices, brown sugar, chile powder, paprika, crushed pepper, hot sauce, onion and garlic powders, cilantro, salt, and black pepper. Mix well.

2. Add the wings to the marinade, coating them thoroughly. Marinate the wings in the refrigerator for 4 hours.

3. Remove the wings from the marinade with tongs and place on a low- to medium-heat grill. Baste and turn for 25 to 30 minutes, or until brown and cooked through.

4. Transfer to a platter and have your lawyer and bail bondsman handy.

CANADIAN MAPLE-LEAF WINGS

☞ **Maple** syrup has more to offer than just a topping for flapjacks! If Canadian syrup is not available, use a pure domestic kind.

½ cup real maple syrup	*2 teaspoons dry mustard*
¼ cup ketchup	*½ teaspoon ground*
1 teaspoon crushed dried	* cinnamon*
* red pepper*	*2 tablespoons (¼ stick)*
¼ cup apple cider vinegar	* unsalted butter*
2 tablespoons grated	*20 trimmed and separated*
* horseradish*	* wings*

1. In a small saucepan over high heat, combine the maple syrup, ketchup, crushed pepper, vinegar, horseradish, mustard, cinnamon, and butter. Bring to a boil and stir until all ingredients are dissolved. Reduce the heat and simmer for 3 minutes. Remove from the heat and let the sauce cool for 5 minutes.

2. Place the wings on a low- to medium-heat grill or barbecue. Brush the wings generously with the basting sauce. Continue to baste and turn the wings for 25 to 30 minutes, or until glazed and cooked through. Transfer to a platter.

CAYMAN ISLAND GRILLED WINGS

☞ **If** you can't travel, create your own little paradise by cooking up these wings in the backyard.

3 tablespoons fresh lime
   juice
2 tablespoons fresh orange
   juice
2 tablespoons canned
   pineapple juice
½ cup canned unsweetened
   coconut milk
2 tablespoons honey

1½ teaspoons lime zest
   (use a zester)
1½ teaspoons orange zest
   (use a zester)
1 teaspoon cayenne pepper
1 teaspoon salt
20 trimmed and separated
   wings

1. In a large mixing bowl, combine the lime, orange, and pineapple juices, coconut milk, honey, lime and orange zests, cayenne, and salt. Mix well.

2. Add the wings to the marinade, coating them thoroughly. Marinate in the refrigerator for 6 hours.

3. Remove the wings from the marinade with tongs and place on a low- to medium-heat grill. Baste and turn frequently for 25 to 30 minutes, or until brown and cooked through.

4. Transfer to a platter, mix the coladas, and apply sunblock.

DESERT FOX WINGS

☞ **This** recipe features the Middle Eastern influences of cumin and cardamom. If General Rommel had supplied his troops with these, they probably could have won the Battle of Alamein.

1/4 cup fresh orange juice
1/2 cup fresh lemon juice
1/4 cup olive oil
4 garlic cloves, minced
1/2 tablespoon lemon zest
  (use a zester)
1/2 tablespoon orange zest
  (use a zester)
2 teaspoons chopped fresh
  rosemary

2 teaspoons dried thyme
2 teaspoons dried oregano
1 teaspoon ground
  cardamom
1 teaspoon ground cumin
1/2 teaspoon turmeric
1/2 teaspoon salt
20 trimmed and separated
  wings

1. In a large mixing bowl, combine the orange and lemon juices, oil, garlic, lemon and orange zests, pepper, rosemary, thyme, oregano, cardamom, cumin, turmeric, and salt. Mix well.

2. Add the wings to the marinade, coating them thoroughly. Let them marinate in the refrigerator for 5 hours.

3. Remove the wings from the marinade with tongs and place on a low- to medium-heat grill or barbecue. Baste and turn frequently for 25 to 30 minutes, or until brown and cooked through.

4. Transfer to a platter and prepare for battle. (If nothing else, you'll have to fight off the neighbors attracted by the aroma of these wings.)

GRINGO WINGS

☞ **You** can find these wings served south of the border in a dirty, dusty little bar by an unshaven bartender with a slim cigar in the corner of his mouth. He will urge you to follow them up with a glass of tequila with a worm. Good luck . . .

2/3 cup fresh lime juice
2/3 cup dry white wine
2 tablespoons tequila
2 teaspoons ground cumin
2 teaspoons chile powder
1 teaspoon salt
1/2 teaspoon ground black
  pepper

2 green chile peppers,
  chopped fine
1/2 cup ketchup
Dash hot sauce
20 trimmed and separated
  wings

1. In a large mixing bowl, combine the lime juice, wine, tequila, cumin, chile powder, salt, pepper, chile peppers, ketchup, and hot sauce. Mix well.

2. Add the wings to the marinade, coating them thoroughly. Let them marinate in the refrigerator for 5 hours.

3. Remove the wings from the marinade with tongs and place on a low- to medium-heat grill. Baste and turn frequently for 25 to 30 minutes, or until brown and cooked through.

4. Transfer to a platter and pour yourself a shot of tequila!

ORIENT MEETS FLORIDA WINGS

☞ **Fusion** cooking has become very popular. Mixing different ethnic foods and techniques creates exciting new dishes.

1/4 cup soy sauce
1/4 cup teriyaki sauce
2 tablespoons red wine
  vinegar
2 teaspoons honey

1 teaspoon light brown
  sugar
1/2 cup fresh orange juice
2 tablespoons orange zest
  (use a zester)

¼ cup vegetable oil
3 tablespoons roasted
    sesame oil
¼ teaspoon crushed dried
    red pepper
1 tablespoon minced fresh
    gingerroot

1 teaspoon toasted sesame
    seeds
20 trimmed and separated
    wings

1. In a large mixing bowl, combine the soy sauce, teriyaki sauce, vinegar, honey, brown sugar, orange juice and zest, vegetable and sesame oils, crushed pepper, ginger, and sesame seeds. Mix well.

2. Add the wings to the marinade, coating them thoroughly. Let wings marinate in the refrigerator for 5 hours.

3. Remove the wings from the marinade with tongs and place on a low- to medium-heat grill. Baste and turn frequently for 25 to 30 minutes, or until brown and cooked through. Transfer to a platter and garnish with orange wedges.

MADE IN JAPAN WINGS

☞ **It's** not only cars, stereos, and sushi that come from the land of the rising sun!

20 trimmed and separated
    wings
¼ cup sake (Japanese
    yellowish rice wine)
3 tablespoons rice wine
    vinegar

2 tablespoons mirin (sweet
    Japanese rice wine)
1 tablespoon Dijon mustard
⅓ cup vegetable oil
1 teaspoon chopped
    shallots

1 teaspoon chopped red
   onion
1 teaspoon (2 cloves)
   minced fresh garlic

2 teaspoons light brown
   sugar
1 teaspoon honey

1. In a large mixing bowl, combine the sake, vinegar, *mirin*, mustard, oil, shallots, onion, garlic, brown sugar, and honey. Mix well.

2. Add the wings to the marinade, coating them thoroughly. Marinate in the refrigerator for 5 hours.

3. Remove the wings from the marinade with tongs and place on a low- to medium-heat grill or barbecue. Baste and turn frequently for 25 to 30 minutes, or until glazed, brown, and cooked through.

4. Transfer to a platter, drink the remaining sake, and accompany the wings with some sushi.

SEÑORITA WINGS

☞ **This** recipe will drive you wild!

1 cup fresh orange juice
½ cup tomato juice
1 small onion, minced
¼ cup chopped green
   onions (scallions)
2 tablespoons tequila

½ teaspoon salt
¼ teaspoon hot sauce
¼ teaspoon sugar
20 trimmed and separated
   wings

1. In a small saucepan over high heat, combine the orange juice, tomato juice, onion, green onions, tequila, salt, hot sauce, and sugar. Stir and bring to a boil, then reduce the heat and simmer for 3 minutes. Remove from the stove and transfer to a large mixing bowl. Let the sauce cool for 1 hour.

2. Add the wings to the cooled marinade, coating them thoroughly. Marinate in the refrigerator for 4 hours.

3. Remove the wings from the marinade with tongs and place on a low- to medium-heat grill or barbecue. Baste and turn for 25 to 30 minutes, or until brown and cooked through.

4. Transfer to a platter and serve with sour cream, salsa, and perhaps a margarita.

SIAM LOTUS WINGS

☞ I like all styles of food, but my favorites are fiery ones, like Thai, Indonesian, and Cajun. This recipe is dedicated to Siam Lotus, a little Thai restaurant on Long Island. They fired up my love for Thai food with their excellent fare.

1 cup canned unsweetened
coconut milk
2 tablespoons fish sauce
(nam pla)
1 tablespoon soy sauce
1½ tablespoons chopped
fresh garlic
½ tablespoon minced fresh
gingerroot
2 tablespoons chopped fresh
cilantro

½ teaspoon crushed dried
red pepper
1 teaspoon ground black
pepper
1 teaspoon turmeric
1 teaspoon curry powder
1 teaspoon fresh lime juice
20 trimmed and separated
wings

1. In a large mixing bowl, combine the coconut milk, fish sauce, soy sauce, garlic, ginger, cilantro, crushed pepper, black pepper, turmeric, curry, and lime juice. Mix well.

2. Add the wings to the marinade, coating them thoroughly. Marinate in the refrigerator for 6 hours.

3. Remove the wings from the marinade with tongs and place on a low- to medium-heat grill. Baste and turn for 25 to 30 minutes, or until brown and cooked through.

4. Transfer to a platter and enjoy with a cold Thai iced tea.

TRIPWIRE WINGS

☞ **These** wings are booby trapped . . . once you try them, the explosion of flavor will send you into an eating frenzy!

¼ cup vegetable oil
1 tablespoon fresh orange
  juice
3 tablespoons fresh lime
  juice
3 tablespoons Triple Sec
  liqueur
2 tablespoons tequila
½ teaspoon lime zest
  (use a zester)
½ teaspoon orange zest
  (use a zester)

½ teaspoon chile powder
½ teaspoon granulated
  sugar
½ teaspoon light brown
  sugar
¼ teaspoon kosher salt
  (use plain salt as
  substitute)
1 jalapeño pepper, chopped
  fine
20 trimmed and separated
  wings

1. In a large mixing bowl, combine the oil, orange and lime juices, Triple Sec, tequila, lime and orange zests, chile powder, granulated sugar, brown sugar, salt, and jalapeño. Mix well.

2. Add the wings to the marinade, coating them thoroughly. Marinate in the refrigerator for 5 hours.

3. Remove the wings from the marinade with tongs and place on a low- to medium-heat grill. Baste and turn for 25 to 30 minutes, or until brown and cooked through.

4. Transfer to a platter and prepare yourself for an explosion of flavors. (Sandbags are available at your local hardware store.)

WHY WORRY CURRY WINGS

☞ **Curry** always brings a mixed reaction. Some worry about curry, assuming it must be hot. Curry is simply a blend of aromatic spices that enhance and color food. When you add hot sauce—well, then the situation changes.

2 tablespoons curry powder
½ teaspoon ground
  cinnamon
¼ teaspoon ground nutmeg
2 tablespoons sweet sherry
¼ cup fresh lime juice
¼ cup fresh lemon juice
¼ cup vegetable oil
2 tablespoons diced red
  onion

¼ cup chopped fresh
  cilantro
1 teaspoon crushed dried
  red pepper
2 teaspoons light brown
  sugar
1 teaspoon honey
20 trimmed and separated
  wings

1. In a large mixing bowl, combine the curry, cinnamon, nutmeg, sherry, lime, lemon, and orange juices, oil, red onion, cilantro, crushed pepper, brown sugar, and honey.

2. Add the wings to the marinade, coating them thoroughly. Marinate in the refrigerator for 5 hours.

3. Remove the wings from the marinade with tongs and place on a low- to medium-heat grill. Baste and turn for 25 to 30 minutes, or until brown and cooked.

4. Transfer to a platter and stop worrying!

WINGS FOR GOODNESS' SAKE

3 tablespoons mirin
  (Japanese rice wine)
*⅓ cup sake (Japanese rice
  wine)*
¼ cup soy sauce
¼ cup dry white wine
1 tablespoon honey

*1 tablespoon light brown
  sugar*
*¼ teaspoon crushed dried
  red pepper*
*20 trimmed and separated
  wings*

1. In a large mixing bowl, combine the *mirin,* sake, soy sauce, wine, honey, brown sugar, and crushed pepper. Mix well.

2. Add the wings to the marinade, coating them thoroughly. Marinate in the refrigerator for 5 hours.

3. Remove the wings from the marinade with tongs and place on a low- to medium-heat grill. Baste and turn for 25 to 30 minutes, or until brown and cooked through.

4. Transfer to a platter and eat more wings, for goodness' sake!

CHICKEN 'N' CHIPS WINGS

☞ **Serve** these wings on newspaper like they serve fish 'n' chips in Britain.

½ cup beer
1 large egg
1 cup all-purpose flour
½ teaspoon salt
¼ teaspoon onion powder
¼ teaspoon turmeric

⅛ teaspoon paprika
Oil, for frying
Flour, for dusting
20 trimmed and separated
   wings

1. Whip the egg and beer in a large mixing bowl until smooth.

2. Fold in the flour, salt, onion powder, turmeric, and paprika. Create a smooth batter, but don't overmix!

3. Let the batter stand for 10 minutes.

4. In a heavy skillet over a high flame, heat 2 inches of frying oil; or heat a deep-fryer with oil to 350° F.

5. Dust the wings with a little flour and dip them one by one into the batter. Important: The batter must stick to the wings and drip off very slowly when each wing is held up. If the batter is too thin, add a little more flour.

6. Drop the wings slowly, one by one, into the oil and fry them until golden brown and cooked through to 165° F, about 12 minutes.

7. Transfer to a platter lined with paper towels to drain. Get out the lemon wedges, newspapers, and tartar sauce . . . and the lager, mate!

CORAL REEF WINGS

☞ **The** papaya in this recipe gives it an exceptional flavor. A papaya is ripe when it feels spongy when pressed.

1 papaya, peeled and diced
1 diced plum tomato
¼ cup diced red onion
1 tablespoon diced shallots
2 jalapeño peppers, seeded
*   and diced*
½ cup apple cider vinegar
2 tablespoons sweet sherry
2 tablespoons dry white
*   wine*
2 tablespoons yellow
*   mustard*
1 tablespoon light brown
*   sugar*

1 tablespoon honey
2 tablespoons
*   Worcestershire sauce*
½ teaspoon hot sauce
½ teaspoon ground allspice
¼ teaspoon crushed dried
*   red pepper*
¼ teaspoon salt
2 tablespoons sweetened
*   shredded coconut*
2 tablespoons vegetable oil
20 trimmed and separated
*   wings*
Dash each salt and pepper

1. In a small saucepan, combine the papaya, diced tomato, onion, shallots, jalapeños, vinegar, sherry, wine, mustard, brown sugar, honey, Worcestershire, hot sauce, allspice, crushed pepper, salt, and shredded coconut.

2. Over high heat, bring the ingredients to a boil, then reduce the heat and simmer for 10 minutes, or until the sauce thickens. Let the sauce cool for 15 minutes.

3. Transfer to a food processor and puree until smooth. Set the sauce aside.

4. In a large skillet, heat the oil over a high flame. Add the wings, sprinkling with salt and pepper to seal in their flavor while they brown. Fry for 10 to 15 minutes, or until brown and cooked through. Remove from the skillet into a large mixing bowl.

5. Add the pureed sauce to the wings and toss, coating the wings thoroughly. Transfer to a platter.

CHILE BABY WINGS

☞ **This** is a South American cooking method applied to many poultry dishes. I think it works great with wings. Enjoy!

*20 trimmed and separated
   wings
4 tablespoons vegetable oil
Pinch each salt and pepper
4 tablespoons cornmeal
4 teaspoons chile powder
2 teaspoons ground cumin
1 cup chopped green onions
   (scallions)*

*4 cups chicken stock
2 teaspoons fresh lime juice
4 ounces canned green
   chiles, chopped
2 cups canned tomatillos,
   drained
½ cup chopped fresh
   cilantro*

1. In a large, heavy skillet, heat the oil over a high flame. Add the chicken wings, sprinkling with salt and pepper to seal in their flavor while you brown them. Fry for 10 to 15 minutes, or until brown and cooked through.

2. Sprinkle the cornmeal, chile powder, cumin, and green onions over the wings, coating them thoroughly.

3. Add the chicken stock, lime juice, chiles, tomatillos, and cilantro. Bring the mixture to a boil over high heat, then reduce the heat and simmer for 5 minutes. Remove from the heat and let the mixture stand for 5 minutes to thicken.

4. Transfer to a platter and serve over rice.

DIANE LOVES WINGS

☞ **This** is a wing variation of the classic steak Diane.

2 tablespoons vegetable oil
20 trimmed and separated
   wings
Dash each salt and pepper
½ cup minced shallots
½ cup brandy

4 teaspoons Dijon mustard
3 teaspoons Worcestershire
   sauce
¼ cup chicken stock
¼ cup (½ stick) unsalted
   butter

1. In a large, heavy skillet, heat the oil over a high flame. Add the wings, sprinkling with salt and pepper to seal in their flavor while they brown. Cook the wings for 10 to 15 minutes, or until brown and cooked through.

2. Add the shallots and cook for 1 minute. Splash the wings with brandy. Ignite and let the flame burn for 3 minutes (for a proper flame, the pan must be hot). Simmer for 3 minutes.

3. Remove the wings from the sauce with tongs. Set aside and keep warm.

4. Whisk the mustard, Worcestershire, chicken stock, and butter into the skillet until smooth. Remove from the heat and pour over the reserved cooked wings. Voilà . . . Wings Diane!

FRIED COCONUT WINGS

☞ **The** wings in this recipe are cooked before they're breaded because the coconut breading browns faster than the chicken can cook internally. The wings are also frozen before they're fried, which helps the breading stick to them and produces a crispier coating.

20 trimmed and separated
   wings
Water, to cover
½ teaspoon salt
½ teaspoon ground black
   pepper

2 cups all-purpose flour
6 large eggs, beaten
1½ cups crushed cornflakes
1½ cups sweetened coconut
   flakes
Vegetable oil, for frying

1. Place the wings in a large pot and cover with cold water. Bring to a boil over a high flame and add the salt and pepper. Reduce the heat and simmer the wings for 10 minutes, or until firm and cooked through. Remove the wings from the water and put on a baking sheet to cool.

2. Set out three large bowls. In the first, place the flour; in the second, the eggs; in the third, combine the cornflakes and coconut. Dip the cooked wings in the flour, then the eggs, then the coconut-cornflake mixture. Place the coated wings on a greased cookie sheet. When all the wings are coated, place the sheet in the freezer for 15 minutes.

3. Heat the vegetable oil in a fryer or a large, heavy skillet to 350° F. Carefully place the wings into the oil one at a time. Fry the wings until they're golden brown and have reached an internal temperature of 165° F (about 12 minutes). Keep in mind that the first batch will cook quickly; adjust the oil temperature if necessary. Drain the wings on a platter lined with paper towels.

4. Enjoy these wings with a piña colada!

HOISIN SCALLION WINGS

☞ **Hoisín** sauce is available in most supermarkets. When you purchase green onions, or scallions, make sure they're firm and crispy.

3 tablespoons vegetable oil
20 trimmed and separated
* wings*
All-purpose flour
Pinch each salt and pepper
½ cup minced onion
2 tablespoons minced fresh
* gingerroot*
3 garlic cloves, sliced thin
½ cup chicken stock

3 tablespoons hoisin *sauce*
½ cup coarsely chopped
* green onions (scallions)*
1 teaspoon hot sauce
2 teaspoons soy sauce
½ teaspoon roasted
* sesame oil*
½ teaspoon crushed dried
* red pepper*
½ teaspoon onion powder

1. In a large, heavy skillet, heat the oil over a high flame. Dust the wings with flour, salt, and pepper, making sure they are lightly coated on all sides. Add the wings carefully to the hot oil and brown for 10 to 12 minutes, or until brown and cooked through. Set aside and keep warm.

2. In the same skillet and with the oil remaining in the pan, sauté the onion, ginger, and garlic until lightly brown and transparent. Deglaze (pour) the pan with chicken stock, scraping to loosen all particles. Add the *hoisin* sauce, green onions, hot sauce, soy sauce, sesame oil, crushed pepper, and onion powder. Bring to a boil over high heat, then reduce the heat and simmer for 2 minutes.

3. Transfer the warm wings to a large mixing bowl. Add the sauce and toss, coating the wings thoroughly. Transfer to a platter and pull out the chopsticks!

GREEN ANGRY LEPRECHAUN WINGS

☞ **Around** St. Patrick's Day, Tabasco introduced a green jalapeño sauce. I dedicate this recipe to all the great Irish pubs serving wings. *Erin go bragh!*

3 tablespoons vegetable oil
20 trimmed and separated wings
Dash each salt and pepper
¼ cup finely chopped onion
1 cup dry white wine
1 tablespoon Dijon mustard
1 tablespoon drained canned green peppercorns (from can)

¼ cup heavy cream
3 stalks diced green onions (scallions)
½ cup chopped fresh parsley
Dash Tabasco green hot sauce
2 tablespoons (¼ stick) unsalted butter

1. In a large, heavy skillet, heat the oil over a high flame. Add the wings, sprinkling with salt and pepper to seal in their flavor while they brown. Fry for 10 minutes, or until brown and cooked through. Remove the wings from the skillet, reserving the oil. Keep the wings warm.

2. In the same skillet over high heat, sauté the onion until tender. Splash with white wine. Add the mustard, peppercorns, and heavy cream. Bring to a boil then reduce the heat and simmer for 3 minutes, or until thickened. Add the green onions and parsley. Whisk in the hot sauce and butter until smooth.

3. Transfer the warm wings to a large mixing bowl. Add the sauce to the wings and toss, coating them thoroughly.

4. Transfer to a platter, wear your green, and tap to the music of *Riverdance.*

GORGONZILLA WINGS

☞ **Gorgonzola** cheese, named for a town outside Milan, Italy, is delicious with salads, dressings, apples, pears, and, yes, chicken wings!

3 tablespoons vegetable oil
20 trimmed and separated
  wings
Pinch each salt and pepper
¼ cup minced red onion

1 tablespoon minced parsley
¼ cup chicken stock
¼ cup heavy cream
¼ cup Gorgonzola cheese

1. In a large, heavy skillet, heat the oil over a high flame. Add the wings, sprinkling with salt and pepper to seal in their flavor while you brown them. Fry for 10 to 12 minutes, or until brown and cooked through. Remove the wings from the pan, reserving the cooking oil. Keep the wings warm.

2. To the same skillet and over high heat, add the red onion and sauté until transparent and tender. Add the chicken stock, parsley, and heavy cream. Bring to a boil then immediately reduce the heat and simmer for 3 minutes, or until the sauce thickens slightly.

3. Fold in the Gorgonzola cheese and stir until it's incorporated.

4. Transfer the warm wings to a large mixing bowl. Add the sauce and toss, making sure the wings are thoroughly coated. Transfer to a platter and watch your favorite Gorgon . . . oops . . . Godzilla movie!

GREEN JUNGLE CURRY WINGS

☞ **The** green curry paste featured in this recipe is used in many Thai dishes. It perfectly complements these wings . . . hot!

95

1 tablespoon coriander
   seeds
1 tablespoon cumin seeds
6 whole peppercorns
3 stalks lemongrass, bulb
   included, minced
½ cup chopped fresh
   cilantro
1 tablespoon minced fresh
   gingerroot
8 whole garlic cloves
1 teaspoon chopped shallots
12 serrano chile peppers,
   seeded

¼ cup water
1 teaspoon salt
1 teaspoon Thai fish sauce
   (nam pla)
1 teaspoon lime zest (use a
   zester)
2 teaspoons fresh lime juice
3 tablespoons vegetable oil
20 trimmed and separated
   wings
1 cup canned unsweetened
   coconut milk

1. To make the green curry paste, toast the cumin and coriander seeds quickly in a medium skillet over a high flame, being careful not to burn them. Combine the toasted cumin and coriander seeds, peppercorns, lemongrass, cilantro, ginger, garlic, shallots, serranos, water, salt, fish sauce, lime zest, and juice in a blender or food processor. Blend and puree until smooth. Set aside.

2. In a large, heavy skillet or wok, heat the oil over a high flame. Add the wings and fry for 10 minutes, or until golden brown and cooked through. Add the coconut milk, bring to a boil, and immediately lower the heat and simmer for 3 to 5 minutes. As soon as the sauce thickens, add the green curry paste to the pan and toss, making sure the wings are thoroughly coated. Remove from the heat.

3. Transfer to a platter, serve with some Basmati rice, and bring out a bottle of Kingfisher Thai beer to soothe the heat.

MULBERRY STREET WINGS

☞ **Mulberry Street,** in Manhattan's Little Italy, is a great place to buy Italian delicacies or to just sit on a hot summer night and enjoy a cup of cappuccino, a great pasta dish, or maybe some Italian wings!

½ cup olive oil
20 trimmed and separated
* wings*
Pinch each salt and pepper
1 teaspoon crushed dried
* red pepper*
8 garlic cloves, cut into thin
* slices*
1 tablespoon chopped fresh
* parsley*

1 tablespoon chopped fresh
* basil*
1 teaspoon chopped fresh
* rosemary*
½ cup diced plum
* tomatoes*
Grated Parmesan, as
* needed*

1. In a large, heavy skillet, heat the oil over a high flame. Add the wings, sprinkling with salt, pepper, and crushed pepper to seal in their flavor while they brown. Add the garlic, parsley, basil, and rosemary. Fry the wings for 10 to 12 minutes, or until brown and cooked through.

2. Transfer to a platter or serve atop your favorite pasta. Sprinkle the chopped tomatoes and cheese over the wings as a garnish.

POLKA POLKA WINGS

☞ **This** could be considered an Eastern European version of chicken wings. It's time for wings to conquer the world.

3 tablespoons vegetable oil
20 trimmed and separated
  wings
Pinch each salt and pepper
1 small onion, diced
½ teaspoon paprika
½ teaspoon onion powder

1 tablespoon chopped fresh
  parsley
1 teaspoon dried dill
½ cup sour cream
¼ cup heavy cream
½ teaspoon grated
  horseradish

1. In a large, heavy skillet, heat the oil over a high flame. Add the wings, sprinkling with salt and pepper to seal in their flavor while they brown. Fry for 10 to 12 minutes, or until brown and firm. Remove the wings from the pan, reserving the oil. Keep the wings warm.

2. In the same pan, sauté the onion over a high flame until golden brown, about 3 minutes. Add the paprika, onion powder, parsley, dill, sour cream, and heavy cream. Whisk until smooth, making sure the mixture does not boil. Once it's hot, remove from the heat.

3. Place the warm wings in a large mixing bowl and pour the sauce over them, coating them thoroughly. Transfer to a platter and enjoy with some polka music and pierogies.

WINGS FRA "DIABLO"

☞ **This** is a "wing version" of a popular Italian dish.

2 tablespoons olive oil
1 tablespoon vegetable oil
20 trimmed and separated
   wings
Dash each salt and pepper
4 garlic cloves, sliced thin
½ cup dry red wine
½ lemon

1 tablespoon chopped fresh
   basil
1 teaspoon dried oregano
1 teaspoon crushed dried
   red pepper
1 (24-ounce) can tomato
   sauce
½ teaspoon sugar

1. In a large, heavy skillet, heat the olive and vegetable oils over a high flame. Add the wings, sprinkling with salt and pepper to seal in their flavor while they brown, about 8 minutes.

2. Add the garlic slices and sauté until they're lightly browned, about 2 minutes. Immediately splash with red wine. Squeeze the juice from the lemon over the wings and simmer for 1 minute. Add the basil, oregano, and crushed pepper.

3. Add the tomato sauce and sugar. Bring to a boil, then reduce the heat and simmer for 10 minutes. If the sauce becomes too thick for your taste, add a little water.

4. Transfer to a platter. You might want to serve these wings with a bowl of spaghetti and some grated cheese.

WING FRIED RICE

☞ **Have** you ever wondered about the origins of fried rice? Way back when, in Asia, leftovers from dinner were kept cool overnight and used at breakfast—where, instead of pancakes, fried rice was served with eggs. Aha!

3 tablespoons vegetable oil
*1 teaspoon roasted
    sesame oil*
*20 trimmed and separated
    wings*
Dash each salt and pepper
5 large eggs
1 tablespoon vegetable oil
*1 teaspoon roasted
    sesame oil*
*3 cups chopped green
    onions (scallions)*

2 cups fresh bean sprouts
*1 green bell pepper, diced
    fine*
*2 red bell peppers, diced
    fine*
*1 tablespoon minced fresh
    gingerroot*
*1 tablespoon minced fresh
    garlic*
3 tablespoons soy sauce
6 cups cooked, hot rice

1. In a large, heavy skillet or wok, heat the sesame and vegetable oils over a high flame. Add the wings, seasoning with salt and pepper to seal in their flavor while they brown. Fry for 10 to 12 minutes, or until brown and cooked through. Remove the wings from the pan and reserve the oil.

2. In the same pan and oil, fry the eggs, breaking the yolks, until well done, about 3 minutes. Remove from the pan. Chop the eggs coarsely and set them aside with the wings.

3. Again in the same pan, heat 1 tablespoon of vegetable oil and 1 teaspoon of sesame oil over a high flame.

4. Sauté the green onions, bean sprouts, red and green peppers, ginger, and garlic until lightly browned and tender, about 3 minutes.

5. Add the reserved chopped eggs and wings, along with the soy sauce and rice. Toss until all the ingredients are incorporated and the rice is a light brown color. Add more soy sauce if you'd like more flavor or saltiness.

6. Transfer to a platter accompanied by some egg rolls and chopsticks . . . and dig in!

WINGS GO MARSALA

☞ **Chicken Marsala**—everybody's favorite chicken dish— is now appearing with chicken wings!

*20 trimmed and separated
   wings
½ cup all-purpose flour
Pinch each salt and pepper
¼ cup vegetable oil
¼ cup finely chopped
   shallots*

*¾ cup Marsala wine
1 cup chicken stock
½ teaspoon lemon juice
¼ cup (½ stick) unsalted
   butter*

1. In a large mixing bowl, dust the wings with flour, salt, and pepper. Toss and shake, making sure the wings are thoroughly coated.

2. In a large, heavy skillet, heat the oil over a high flame. Add the wings and fry for 3 minutes or until golden brown, continuously scraping the bottom of the pan to make sure the flour doesn't stick.

3. Add the shallots and sauté for 2 minutes. Splash the wings with Marsala and ignite, if you like, or simply simmer for 5 minutes.

4. Add the chicken stock and lemon juice and bring to a boil. Immediately lower the heat and simmer the wings for 5 to 8 minutes, or until the sauce thickens.

5. Turn off the heat and remove the wings from the sauce with tongs. Quickly whisk in the butter until smooth. Return the wings to the pan and toss, making sure they're thoroughly coated with sauce. Transfer to a platter and surprise your friends and neighbors!

WINGS ACROSS HUNGARY

☞ **A** favorite dish of mine is the Hungarian ethnic dish called Chicken Paprikash. At the Heidelberg Cafe on Manhattan's Eighty-Sixth Street, they serve a great one over homemade späetzle (egg noodles). I figured this would work great with wings. It does. Try this wing recipe with egg noodles and a cold glass of beer.

¼ cup vegetable oil
20 trimmed and separated
*   wings*
Pinch each salt and pepper
1 teaspoon paprika
2 small onions, sliced thin
½ teaspoon sugar

¾ cup dry white wine
1 teaspoon hot sauce
2 teaspoons paprika
½ teaspoon fresh or dried
*   dill*
½ cup sour cream

1. In a large, heavy skillet, heat the oil over a high flame. Add the wings, sprinkling with salt, pepper, and paprika to seal in their flavor and color.

2. Fry the wings for 12 minutes, or until golden brown and cooked through. Remove from the pan, set aside, and keep warm.

3. In the same pan, sauté the onions in the remaining oil until golden brown. Add the sugar, wine, hot sauce, and spices. Simmer for 2 minutes. Whip in the sour cream. Add the reserved wings to the sauce and simmer for about 5 minutes until the sauce thickens. Transfer to a platter.

WINGS AU PARIS

☞ **This** recipe is a derivation of the famous French dish Steak au Poivre. It's a popular entrée in many French bistros.

*20 trimmed and separated
   wings
¼ cup olive oil
1 teaspoon coarse kosher or
   sea salt
2 tablespoons cracked black
   pepper
¼ cup vegetable oil
½ cup minced shallots
3 tablespoons brandy*

*¾ cup dry white wine
1 teaspoon dried tarragon
½ cup chicken stock
1 teaspoon green
   peppercorns
3 tablespoons chopped fresh
   parsley
¼ cup heavy cream
2 tablespoons (¼ stick)
   unsalted butter*

1. In a large mixing bowl, combine the wings, olive oil, salt, and cracked black pepper. Press the pepper into the wings to coat them as thorough as possible.

2. In a large, heavy skillet, heat the vegetable oil over a high flame. Add the wings and fry for 8 minutes until golden brown, making sure the pepper is seared in for flavor. Add the shallots and sauté for 1 minute, or until transparent.

3. Splash the wings with brandy and ignite, if you wish, or simmer for 5 minutes. Splash with white wine. Add the tarragon, chicken stock, and green peppercorns. Simmer for 3 to 5 minutes, or until the sauce starts to thicken. Remove the wings from sauce and set them aside.

4. Quickly whisk the parsley, cream, and butter into the sauce. Return the wings to the pan, coating them thoroughly with sauce. Transfer to a platter and enjoy with a glass of red wine.

ARUGULA-PESTO WINGS

☞ **This** is a light wing recipe, perfect to bring along on a summer picnic.

2 tablespoons olive oil
3 large garlic cloves
1/3 cup feta cheese
1/3 cup low-fat cream cheese
2 green onion (scallion) stalks, coarsely chopped
1/2 teaspoon fresh lemon juice

1/2 teaspoon onion powder
1/2 teaspoon ground black pepper
1 large bunch arugula, de-rooted and washed
20 trimmed and separated wings
Pinch each salt and pepper

1. Preheat the oven to 375° F.

2. In a small skillet, heat the olive oil over a medium flame. Add the garlic cloves and brown lightly for 2 minutes, making sure they don't burn (burned garlic tastes bitter).

3. Remove the pan from the heat and pour the oil and garlic into a blender or food processor. Let them cool for 5 minutes. Add the feta, cream cheese, and green onions; puree until smooth.

4. Add the lemon juice, onion powder, and pepper; puree.

5. With a knife, coarsely chop the arugula. Add to the blender or food processor. Blend, making sure the arugula is still a little chunky (do not puree). Add salt, if needed. With a rubber spatula, transfer the mixture to a large mixing bowl and set aside.

6. Spread the wings evenly on a buttered 2-inch-deep baking dish. Sprinkle with salt and pepper to enhance their flavor while they bake.

7. Bake the wings, turning them occasionally and brushing them with olive oil, for 25 to 30 minutes, or until brown and cooked through. Remove from the oven and let them cool to just semihot.

8. Add the wings to the sauce in the bowl with tongs while shaking off any excess oil. Toss with the arugula-pesto mixture, making sure they are thoroughly coated.

9. Transfer to a platter or picnicware and serve with crusty sourdough bread.

BAVARIAN OOM-PAH-PAH WINGS

☞ **Now** here is an Oktoberfest wing recipe, great with beer and a few slices of pumpernickel bread.

1/4 cup coarse German mustard
2 tablespoons honey
1 teaspoon dry mustard
1 teaspoon onion powder
2 tablespoons beer
1 teaspoon apple cider vinegar

1/4 teaspoon cayenne pepper
1/4 teaspoon garlic powder
1/2 teaspoon ground black pepper
1/4 cup chopped green onions (scallions)
20 trimmed and separated wings

1. Preheat the oven to 350° F.

2. In a large mixing bowl, combine the mustard, honey, dry mustard, onion powder, beer, vinegar, cayenne, garlic, pepper, and green onions.

3. Add the wings to the bowl and toss, making sure they're thoroughly coated. Marinate for 4 hours in the refrigerator.

4. Spread the wings evenly on a buttered 2-inch-deep baking dish and bake for 25 to 30 minutes, turning occasionally, until the wings are brown and cooked through. Transfer to a platter and . . . prosit!

BOMBAY EXPRESS WINGS

☞ **This** is a refreshing recipe for summertime. The yogurt gives the chicken a great tangy flavor.

1 tablespoon chopped fresh cilantro	1 teaspoon curry powder
½ teaspoon crushed dried red pepper	1 teaspoon sugar
½ cup chopped green onions (scallions)	½ teaspoon salt
	1 cup yogurt
	20 trimmed and separated wings

1. In a large mixing bowl, combine the cilantro, crushed pepper, green onions, curry, sugar, salt, and yogurt. Mix well.

2. Add the wings, coating them thoroughly. Marinate in the refrigerator for 4 hours.

3. Preheat the oven to 350° F. Spread the wings evenly on a buttered 2-inch-deep baking dish and bake for 25 to 30 minutes, or until brown and cooked through. Transfer to a platter and serve with pita bread.

CRUSOE BAKED WINGS

☞ I hope you enjoy this tropical wing recipe as much as Robinson Crusoe did!

1 cup unsalted butter, melted
1 teaspoon fresh lime juice
1 teaspoon canned
*   pineapple juice*
2 garlic cloves, minced
¼ teaspoon hot sauce
1 cup plain bread crumbs
1 tablespoon chopped fresh
*   parsley*

1 teaspoon paprika
1 teaspoon ground black
*   pepper*
½ teaspoon salt
½ teaspoon onion powder
⅛ teaspoon ground allspice
20 trimmed and separated
*   wings*

1. Preheat the oven to 350° F.

2. In a small mixing bowl, whisk the butter, lime and pineapple juices, garlic, and hot sauce. Mix well and set aside.

3. In a separate, large mixing bowl, combine the bread crumbs, parsley, paprika, pepper, salt, onion powder, and allspice. Mix well.

4. Dip the wings one at a time into the sauce, then press each wing into the bread crumb mixture. Make sure the wings are thoroughly coated with the bread crumb mixture.

5. Spread the wings evenly on a buttered 2-inch-deep baking dish and bake for 25 to 30 minutes, turning occasionally, until brown, crispy, and cooked through.

6. Transfer to a platter, crack a coconut, and enjoy under the palm tree.

DEVIL'S ISLAND CHICKEN WINGS

1 tablespoon olive oil
1 small onion, finely diced
1 garlic clove, minced
1 jalapeño pepper, seeded
  and minced
½ teaspoon minced fresh
  gingerroot
½ teaspoon chile powder
½ teaspoon paprika

¼ teaspoon cayenne pepper
¼ cup red wine vinegar
½ cup ketchup
2 tablespoons light brown
  sugar
2 tablespoons hot sauce
2 teaspoons Dijon mustard
20 trimmed and separated
  wings

1. Preheat the oven to 350° F.

2. In a medium saucepan, heat the oil over a medium flame. Add the onion, garlic, and jalapeño. Sauté for 3 minutes, or until tender and transparent. Add the ginger, chile powder, paprika, and cayenne. Mix well.

3. Add the vinegar, ketchup, brown sugar, hot sauce, and mustard. Bring to a simmer and stir for 5 minutes. Remove from the heat and transfer to a large mixing bowl. Let the mixture cool for 10 minutes.

4. Add the wings to the sauce, coating them thoroughly. With tongs, transfer the wings to a buttered 2-inch-deep baking dish, spreading them evenly.

5. Bake for 25 to 30 minutes, turning occasionally, until brown and cooked through.

INDO SATAY WINGS

☞ **In** Holland, where I grew up, Indonesian cuisine is as popular as Chinese cuisine is in the United States. You can buy a snack of chicken satay from carts on street corners or in snack bars. The peanut sauce featured in this recipe is also widely used in various dishes from Malaysia and Thailand.

¼ cup chunky peanut butter
2 teaspoons curry powder
½ teaspoon onion powder
½ teaspoon salt
½ teaspoon ground black pepper
½ tablespoon light brown sugar
3 tablespoons soy sauce

2 teaspoons chopped fresh cilantro
2 tablespoons (10 cloves) chopped fresh garlic
2 tablespoons canned pineapple juice
½ tablespoon hot sauce
20 trimmed and separated wings

1. In a large mixing bowl, combine the peanut butter, curry, onion powder, salt, pepper, brown sugar, honey, soy sauce, cilantro, garlic, pineapple juice, and hot sauce. Mix well.

2. Add the wings to the bowl, coating them thoroughly. Marinate the wings in the refrigerator for 4 hours.

3. Preheat the oven to 350° F. With tongs, spread the wings evenly on a buttered 2-inch-deep baking dish and bake wings for 25 to 30 minutes, turning occasionally, until brown and cooked through. Transfer to a platter.

CASTAWAY WINGS

⅔ cup canned unsweetened
   coconut milk
½ cup orange marmalade
¼ cup fresh lime juice
¼ cup canned pineapple
   juice
2 teaspoons Worcestershire
   sauce
1 teaspoon hot sauce

½ cup grated sweetened
   coconut
3 garlic cloves, minced
½ teaspoon ground black
   pepper
1 tablespoon chopped fresh
   cilantro
20 trimmed and separated
   wings

1. In a small saucepan over a high flame, heat the coconut milk and orange marmalade until the marmalade dissolves. Add the lime and pineapple juices, Worcestershire, hot sauce, coconut, garlic, pepper, and cilantro. Stir until hot; do not boil. Turn off the heat.

2. Transfer the mixture to a large mixing bowl and let it cool for 20 minutes. Add the wings and marinate for 4 hours in the refrigerator.

3. Preheat the oven to 350° F. Remove the wings from the marinade with tongs and spread evenly on a buttered 2-inch-deep baking dish.

4. Bake for 25 to 30 minutes, turning occasionally, until brown, glazed, and cooked through. Transfer to a platter.

LORD CHUTNEY WINGS

½ cup mango chutney
(available in most
supermarkets)
1 tablespoon Grey Poupon
mustard

Juice of ½ orange
2 tablespoons (¼ stick)
unsalted butter, melted
20 trimmed and separated
wings

1. Preheat the oven to 350° F.

2. In a large mixing bowl, combine the chutney, mustard, orange juice, and butter. Mix well.

3. Add the wings to the mixture, coating them thoroughly. With tongs, spread the wings evenly on a buttered 2-inch-deep baking dish.

4. Bake for 20 to 25 minutes, or until golden brown and cooked through. Turn occasionally to prevent sticking.

5. Transfer to a silver platter and have the butler serve your honored guests.

MANGO TANGO WINGS

☞ **Do** you love mango and papaya like I do? Try this recipe and be the papaya king!

1 ripe mango, peeled,
    pitted, and chopped
    coarsely
1 ripe papaya, peeled,
    seeded, and chopped
1 habañero pepper, seeded
    and chopped
1 tablespoon dark rum
1 teaspoon hot sauce
1 tablespoon grated fresh
    gingerroot

½ teaspoon ground
    coriander
¼ teaspoon turmeric
¼ teaspoon ground cumin
½ cup unsweetened coconut
    milk
¼ cup fresh lime juice
1 tablespoon chopped fresh
    cilantro
20 trimmed and separated
    wings

1. In a food processor or blender, combine the mango, papaya, and habañero. Pulse and puree until smooth. Transfer with a rubber spatula into a small saucepan. Add the rum, hot sauce, ginger, coriander, turmeric, cumin, coconut milk, lime juice, and cilantro. Over a medium flame, bring the mixture to a simmer. Mix and stir well for 3 minutes.

2. Remove the pan from the stove and pour into a large mixing bowl. Let the mixture cool for 20 minutes. Add the wings and marinate for 6 hours in the refrigerator.

3. Preheat the oven to 350° F.

4. With tongs, remove the wings from the marinade and spread evenly on a buttered 2-inch-deep baking dish.

5. Bake for 25 to 30 minutes, turning occasionally, until brown and cooked through. Transfer to a platter and do the mango tango!

BARBARIAN HORSEMAN WINGS

☞ **These** wings were the staple of warriors on the battlefield. Legend says it gave them invincible strength.

20 trimmed and separated
  wings
1 cup hoisin *sauce*
½ cup rice wine vinegar
½ cup honey
1 tablespoon light brown
  sugar

1 teaspoon minced shallots
1 teaspoon roasted sesame oil
1 teaspoon crushed dried
  red pepper
½ teaspoon ground white
  pepper
½ teaspoon onion powder

1. In a large mixing bowl, combine the *hoisin* sauce, vinegar, honey, brown sugar, shallots, sesame oil, crushed pepper, white pepper, and onion powder. Mix well.

2. Add the wings to the marinade, coating them thoroughly. Marinate for 4 hours in the refrigerator.

3. Preheat the oven to 350° F. Evenly spread the wings on a buttered 2-inch-deep baking dish.

4. Bake for 25 to 30 minutes, turning occasionally, until brown, glazed, and cooked through.

5. Transfer to a platter. May the Gods of the Plains be with you in strength and power.

OLÉ MOLÉ WINGS

☞ **Chocolate** with wings? Trust me, you'll be surprised at how delicious this is.

20 trimmed and separated
    wings
2 tablespoons (10 cloves)
    minced fresh garlic
1 small onion, minced
1 tablespoon sesame seeds
1 teaspoon crushed dried
    red pepper
1 (8-inch) corn tortilla, torn
    into pieces
1 tablespoon raisins
½ teaspoon ground cloves
1 teaspoon fresh cilantro

¼ teaspoon cinnamon
¼ teaspoon salt
½ teaspoon onion powder
1 ounce unsweetened
    chocolate, grated
1 teaspoon granulated
    sugar
½ teaspoon light brown
    sugar
1 (28-ounce) can crushed
    tomatoes
1 cup chicken stock

1. Preheat the oven to 375° F.

2. Spread the wings evenly on a greased 2-inch-deep baking dish and bake for 25 to 30 minutes, turning occasionally, until they are brown and cooked through. Transfer the wings to a large mixing bowl and keep warm.

3. In a food processor or blender, combine the garlic, onion, sesame seeds, crushed pepper, tortilla, raisins, cloves, cilantro, cinnamon, salt, and onion powder. Blend until smooth.

4. Pour the mixture into a saucepan and bring to a simmer over a medium flame. Add the grated chocolate, granulated sugar, and brown sugar. Stir vigorously until the chocolate and sugars are incorporated. Add the crushed tomatoes and chicken stock. Continue to simmer, stirring occasionally, for 30 to 35 minutes.

5. Transfer the sauce to the bowl containing the wings, and toss to thoroughly coat. Serve on a platter and call your chocoholic friends to join you for a chocolate adventure!

ONION-CILANTRO WINGS

☞ **Cilantro** is a wonderful herb when used with wings; it appears in many of the recipes throughout this book. Cilantro has a pungent, lively fragrance and is mostly used in southwestern, Asian, and Caribbean cooking. If you buy a fresh bunch and can't use all of it, place the cilantro in a glass of water, roots down, into the refrigerator. Cover it with a plastic bag to avoid the cold refrigerator air. Change the water every few days.

½ cup finely chopped onion
½ cup finely chopped red onion
½ cup chopped fresh cilantro
¼ teaspoon salt
¼ teaspoon ground black pepper
⅛ teaspoon hot sauce

2 tablespoons olive oil
1 tablespoon fresh lime juice
1 tablespoon fresh lemon juice
1 tablespoon sugar
20 trimmed and separated wings

1. In a food processor or blender, combine the onion, red onion, cilantro, salt, pepper, hot sauce, olive oil, lime and lemon juices, and sugar. Blend until pureed. Transfer with a rubber spatula to a large mixing bowl.

2. Add the wings, coating them thoroughly. Marinate in the refrigerator for 4 hours.

3. Preheat the oven to 350° F. With tongs, spread the wings evenly on a buttered 2-inch-deep baking dish. Bake for 25 to 30 minutes, or until brown and cooked through. Transfer to a platter.

SIMPLY TERIYAKI WINGS

☞ **Teriyaki** is one of the most popular marinades for all kinds of meat. How could I possibly omit it?

½ cup teriyaki sauce
½ cup vegetable oil
¼ cup dry white wine
4 teaspoons minced fresh
gingerroot

2 teaspoons granulated sugar
1 teaspoon light brown sugar
2 garlic cloves, minced
20 trimmed and separated
wings

1. In a small saucepan over medium heat, combine the teriyaki sauce, oil, wine, ginger, granulated sugar, brown sugar, and garlic. Heat until the sugars are dissolved. Remove from the flame and let the mixture cool for 10 minutes.

2. In a large mixing bowl, toss the wings and marinade together, making sure the wings are thoroughly coated. Marinate for 4 hours in the refrigerator.

3. Preheat the oven to 350° F. With tongs, evenly spread the wings on a buttered 2-inch-deep baking dish.

4. Bake for 25 to 30 minutes, turning occasionally, until brown, glazed, and cooked through. Transfer to a platter.

WINGS TANDOORI

☞ **This** is a yummy Indian-style wing recipe; serve it with Tandoori-style flat bread.

½ cup yogurt
2 garlic cloves, minced
1 teaspoon ground
   coriander
1 teaspoon chopped fresh
   mint
½ teaspoon turmeric
¼ teaspoon saffron threads
¼ teaspoon salt
¼ teaspoon paprika

1 teaspoon sugar
¼ teaspoon cayenne pepper
¼ cup chopped fresh
   cilantro
¼ cup chopped red onion
½ tablespoon fresh lime
   juice
20 trimmed and separated
   wings

1. In a large mixing bowl, combine the yogurt, garlic, coriander, mint, turmeric, saffron, salt, paprika, sugar, cayenne, cilantro, red onion, and lime juice. Mix well.

2. Add the wings, coating them thoroughly. Marinate for 5 hours in the refrigerator.

3. Preheat the oven to 350° F. Spread the wings evenly on a buttered 2-inch-deep baking dish.

4. Bake for 25 to 30 minutes, turning occasionally, until golden brown and cooked through. Transfer to a platter.

TORTILLA JACKET WINGS

☞ **Crushed** tortilla chips make a fabulous crust. This technique works for fish, pork, and beef as well as wings!

2 cups crushed tortilla chips
2 teaspoons chile powder
¼ teaspoon onion powder
¼ teaspoon garlic powder
1 tablespoon chopped fresh
  cilantro

4 large eggs
1 cup milk
20 trimmed and separated
  wings

1. Preheat the oven to 350° F.

2. In a large mixing bowl, combine the tortilla chips, chile powder, onion powder, garlic powder, and cilantro. Mix well and set aside.

3. In a large bowl, whisk the eggs and milk. Set aside.

4. Dip the wings one at a time into the egg mixture, then into the breading mixture, making sure they're thoroughly coated.

5. Spread the wings evenly on a buttered 2-inch-deep baking dish and bake for 25 to 30 minutes, turning occasionally, until brown, crispy, and cooked through. Transfer to a platter and serve with salsa and sour cream.

GREAT WINGS OF ASTORIA

☞ **Astoría,** Queens, New York; the Greek food capital of America. It's a wonderful area to buy authentic Mediterranean foods.

2 tablespoons olive oil
2 tablespoons fresh lemon
 juice
1 tablespoon (5 cloves)
 chopped fresh garlic
1 teaspoon salt
½ teaspoon ground black
 pepper
½ teaspoon dried oregano

1 teaspoon chopped fresh
 dill
¼ teaspoon onion powder
¼ teaspoon garlic powder
½ teaspoon sugar
1 tablespoon chopped fresh
 parsley
20 trimmed and separated
 wings

1. In a large mixing bowl, combine the olive oil, lemon juice, garlic, salt, pepper, oregano, dill, onion and garlic powders, sugar, and parsley. Mix well.

2. Add the wings, coating them thoroughly. Marinate for 4 hours in the refrigerator.

3. Preheat the oven to 350° F. Evenly spread the wings on a buttered 2-inch-deep baking dish. Reserve the marinade.

4. Bake the wings 25 to 30 minutes, occasionally turning and basting with the reserved marinade, until they're brown and cooked through. Sprinkle some feta cheese over them, if you like.

5. Transfer to a platter accompanied by Greek olives and feta cheese.

WING JOINTS

This chapter features recipes from famous chicken-wing kitchens around the country.

BAJA FIRE WINGS

☞ **The** Baja Grill is a restaurant that recently opened a location in East Northport, New York. What impresses me most about this place is their refreshing approach to southwestern food.

½ cup all-purpose flour
½ teaspoon chile powder
20 trimmed and separated
 wings
¼ cup vegetable oil
1 cup Cilantro Lime
 Dressing (see below)

½ cup Frank's REDHOT
 Sauce (or other extra-hot
 sauce)
¼ cup habañero sauce
2 tablespoons (¼ stick)
 unsalted butter

1. In a large mixing bowl, combine the flour, chile powder, and wings. Thoroughly coat the wings with flour.

2. In a large, heavy skillet, heat the oil over a high flame. Add the wings and pan-fry for 10 to 15 minutes, or until crispy, brown, and cooked through.

3. Drain the excess oil from the pan. Add the hot sauce, habañero sauce, and butter. Toss thoroughly until the wings are evenly coated.

4. Transfer the wings to a pineapple-garnished platter with Cilantro Lime Dressing.

CILANTRO LIME DRESSING

1 cup bottled ranch dressing
1 teaspoon chopped fresh
   cilantro

1 teaspoon fresh lime juice

Combine the ranch dressing, cilantro, and lime juice in a small mixing bowl. Mix well.

ORANGE HONEY BARBECUE WINGS

☞ **Frank** Liotta is a 1981 Culinary Institute of America graduate and is currently the executive chef at the New Image Cafe, located at the Olympus-America headquarters in Melville, New York. He submitted this delicious recipe, which he serves to his corporate guests.

1 cup ketchup
2 tablespoons fresh orange
   juice
2 tablespoons honey
1 teaspoon dried ginger
½ teaspoon Liquid Smoke
   or 1 teaspoon mesquite
   seasoning

2 tablespoons red wine
   vinegar
2 tablespoons sugar
Dash Tabasco sauce
20 trimmed and separated
   wings

1. In a large mixing bowl, combine the ketchup, orange juice, honey, ginger, Liquid Smoke, vinegar, sugar, and Tabasco. Mix well.

2. Add the wings, coating them thoroughly. Marinate in the refrigerator for 2 hours.

3. Remove the wings from the marinade with tongs and place on a low- to medium-heat grill. Baste frequently with the remaining marinade.

4. Grill the wings for 20 to 25 minutes, or until they are brown, glazed, and cooked through. Transfer to a platter.

WING HOT SPOT: PLUCK-U

Pluck U is a popular wing chain with four locations in Manhattan. Their chicken wings have been voted number one in New York three years in a row.

While in college, owners Steve and Greg decided to forgo careers on Wall Street for selling Buffalo-style wings in New York City. They decided, in other words, to "wing it."

The two pluckers set out armed with a little ingenuity, determination, and mom's chicken-wing recipe. From there they developed their five secret sauces: mild, medium, hot, 2 hot death, and BBQ.

And so, on August 31, 1989, Pluck University was born!

WING HOT SPOT: WINGS OF GLORY

Wings of Glory is a great Buffalo-wing restaurant and catering company owned by Cedric and Patricia Singleterry.

They opened the restaurant in August '95, and quickly established a huge following due to their unique approach of elevating wings to a main entrée, as opposed to an appetizer.

They have two styles: Cajun wings (marinated, Cajun seasoned, and fried with a light crunchy coating) and New York wings (marinated, seasoned, and tossed with the sauce of your choice). Wings of Glory offers fourteen flavors: mild, hot, suicide, Texas heat, honey barbecue, hot honey barbecue, honey mustard, teriyaki, sweet 'n' sour, honey lemon, Jamaican, barbecue, Hawaiian, and garlic lemon pepper. Their unique marinating process produces a juicy wing.

WINGS OF GLORY SUICIDE WINGS

☞ **Here's** one of Terry and Cedric Singleterry's great wing recipes. (Have a lot of water ready!)

Vegetable oil, for frying	6 tablespoons cayenne
20 trimmed and separated	pepper
wings	4 habañero peppers, seeded
1 cup Frank's Red Hot	and finely chopped
cayenne pepper sauce (or	2 tablespoons ground black
any brand of extra-hot	pepper
sauce)	

1. In a deep-fryer, heat the oil to 350° F. Add the wings and fry until crispy, brown, and no longer pink in the center, about 12 minutes. Drain well on paper towels.

2. In a large mixing bowl, combine the hot sauce, cayenne, habañeros, and pepper. Mix well.

3. Transfer the wings to the mixing bowl and toss, making sure they're thoroughly coated.

4. Transfer the wings to a platter, serve with blue cheese and celery sticks, and . . . burn alive!

HOT SPOT: TOTALLY WINGS

Owner Larry Leinwand opened Totally Wings a few years back. His job as an accountant was boring and selling wings was a more exciting way to earn a living. He decided to open his venture in Huntington Village, New York. The town's club scene is popular on weekends, packed with students from all over. by staying open late, Larry swiftly built up a reputation among hungry clubgoers.

TOTALLY WINGS BUFFALO PIZZA

☞ **In** addition to delicious wings, Larry Leinwand has created some interesting hot dishes at Totally Wings.

¼ cup Durkee hot sauce
  (or a similar kind)
⅛ teaspoon garlic powder
Pinch cayenne pepper

1 (4-ounce) chicken cutlet
¼ cup crumbled blue cheese
1 nonpocket pita

1. In a medium mixing bowl, combine the hot sauce, garlic powder, and cayenne. Mix well. Add the chicken cutlet and marinate in the refrigerator for 2 hours.

2. Preheat the oven to 350° F. Remove the cutlet from the marinade and place on a grill or barbecue over high heat. Remove the cutlet when it's cooked through, and dice into 1-inch pieces. Mix with the blue cheese in a bowl. Sprinkle with a little hot sauce.

3. Top the pita with the chicken mixture, place on a greased baking pan, and bake for 5 to 8 minutes, or until the cheese is melted.

Serves 1 to 2.

WING HOT SPOT: YAK-ZIES BAR & GRILL

Yak-Zies Bar & Grill in Chicago is *the* place for wings in good old Chicago-town.

Joe Spagnoli and his wife, Lisa, sell wings in three different locations. Between them all, the couple sell twelve tons of wings a week.

I visited one location adjacent to famous Wrigley Field. The wings were delicious, but Joe would not part with his secret recipe. He only revealed that the sauce contains nine different ingredients!

The wings are offered in mild, medium, hot, and "Oh My Gosh!"

WING HOT SPOT: BUFFALO WILD WINGS (BW-3) BAR AND GRILL

BW-3, Inc., headquartered in Minneapolis, operates eleven company-owned restaurants and has franchised sixty-one restaurants in fourteen states under the trade name BW-3 Grill and Pub, and more recently under the name Buffalo Wild Wings and Bar.

Soaring high on Buffalo wings, the BW-3 story begins one evening in 1981. Jim Disbrow and Scott Lowery were craving spicy Buffalo-style chicken wings. After scouring Kent, Ohio, they came up empty handed and hungry, so they cooked up an idea: a fun, friendly restaurant with great wings at affordable prices. Their initial store at Ohio State University was wildly successful.

The secret to their success is the twelve sauces, each uniquely flavored, from the mildest teriyaki sauce to the better-be-ready, blazing Buffalo Wild Wing sauce.

Many wings later, BW-3 has walked away with Best Wings awards from leading Midwest magazines and newspapers. Congrats!

TOMMY'S TIGER WINGS

☞ **This** recipe was submitted by a very good friend of mine, Tommy Dimonti, the chef at the Dog and Duck restaurant in Sayville, New York. This restaurant is notorious for its gigantic beer selection and, of course, fabulous wings.

½ cup cold water	All-purpose flour, for
1 cup all-purpose flour	dusting
1 large egg	2 cups crushed cornflakes
Pinch baking powder	Vegetable oil, for frying
20 trimmed and separated	
wings	

1. In a large mixing bowl, combine the water, flour, egg, and baking powder. Beat well, creating a smooth, thick batter. The batter should stick to and lightly coat the spoon. Set aside.

2. Dust the wings with flour. Shake off excess flour and dip the wings into the batter, making sure they're thoroughly coated. Roll the battered wings in the cornflakes; place them on a cookie sheet, cover them with plastic wrap, and put them in the freezer for 2 hours. (Freezing helps cut down on breading loss when frying.)

3. Preheat the oven to 350° F. Heat 2 inches of vegetable oil in a large, heavy skillet over a high flame, or heat the oil in a fryer to 350° F. Carefully place the semifrozen wings in the hot oil. Turn the wings often to prevent burning, and remove them from the oil when they're golden brown (after about 5 minutes).

4. Spread the wings evenly on a baking sheet and bake for 10 more minutes. Remove from the oven and serve on a platter garnished with pineapple and orange slices.

WILD DRAGON WINGS

☞ **The** following recipe was created by chef Michael Morrison (a.k.a. Captain Chaos), a freelancer who cooks and creates ice carvings for New York caterers Thatch Cottage and Culinary Events. He created these wings, aided by plentiful beer, on the eve of my birthday.

¼ cup melted butter
2 cups all-purpose flour
1 teaspoon baking soda
¼ cup chopped fresh parsley
1 cup hot sauce
20 trimmed and separated
   wings
¼ cup roasted sesame oil
¼ cup diced shallots

1 small red onion, minced
1 diced red chile pepper
¼ cup dry white wine
1 cup beef stock (made from
   a bouillon cube)
1 cup tomato puree
Chinese fried noodles (for
   garnish)

1. Preheat the oven to 350° F.

2. In a large mixing bowl, combine the flour, baking soda, and parsley; mix well. Set aside.

3. In a medium mixing bowl, whisk the hot sauce and melted butter. Add the wings, coating them thoroughly.

4. Dip the coated wings into the flour mixture, then remove, shaking off the excess. Set aside.

5. In a large, heavy skillet, heat the vegetable oil over a high flame. Add the wings and fry for 5 to 8 minutes, or until golden brown. Transfer the wings to a baking sheet and bake for 10 minutes to cook the wings internally. Remove from the oven and keep warm.

6. In the meantime, prepare the sauce by heating the sesame oil in a small saucepan. Sauté the shallots, red onions, and red chile pepper for 3 minutes, or until translucent. Add the wine and simmer for an additional 3 minutes. Add the beef stock and tomato puree and stir well over a low flame for 10 minutes. Remove from the stove and transfer to a large mixing bowl. Add the wings and toss, making sure they're thoroughly coated.

7. Transfer to a platter and sprinkle with Chinese fried noodles.

YUKON JACK SNAKEBITE WINGS

☞ **Here's** another recipe from Michael Morrison that includes an ingenious way to use everyone's favorite liquor in a great wing dish! Just make sure you have a designated driver handy.

½ cup vegetable oil, divided
1 teaspoon salt
1 teaspoon chile powder
2 teaspoons crushed dried red pepper
¼ cup sugar

20 trimmed and separated wings
½ cup Yukon Jack Snakebite liquor
¼ cup hot sauce of your choice

1. In a large mixing bowl, combine 1/4 cup of vegetable oil with the salt, chile powder, crushed pepper, and sugar. Mix well.

2. Add the wings, coating them thoroughly.

3. In a large, heavy skillet, heat the remaining 1/4 cup of oil over a high flame. Add the wings and fry for 10 to 12 minutes, or until golden brown and cooked through. Splash with Yukon Jack and simmer for 3 minutes. Add the hot sauce and toss to coat. Ready to serve!

BUFOLOO KILLER WINGS

☞ **The** following recipe was created during a photo shoot at Skippers Pub in Northport, New York, the shooting location of the motion picture *In and Out,* starring Kevin Kline and Tom Selleck. Chef Salomon Caldeira created this one with me. With its ingredients, it should be able to kill a buffalo! I present here a milder version for your safety. (Special thanks to owner Paul Gallowitsch for risking his kitchen for this experiment.)

¼ cup vegetable oil
20 trimmed and separated
  wings
½ teaspoon salt
2 teaspoons cracked black
  pepper
1 teaspoon (2 cloves)
  chopped fresh garlic
⅛ cup Jack Daniels whiskey
  (1 shot)

1 teaspoon grated
  horseradish
1 teaspoon dried parsley
¼ cup chicken stock
1 tablespoon grated
  Parmesan or pecorino
  cheese
¾ cup hot sauce

1. In a large, heavy skillet, heat the oil over a high flame. Add the wings, sprinkling with salt and pepper to seal in their flavor. Cool the wings for 10 minutes, or until brown. Add the garlic and brown for 2 minutes. Splash with Jack Daniels. Ignite the alcohol if you wish and let the flames burn out, or simmer for 3 minutes.

2. Add the horseradish, parsley, chicken stock, and cheese; stir. Add the hot sauce and toss the wings until they're glazed with the sauce.

3. Transfer to a platter, fetch a bucket of water, and get ready for a sinus-clearing experience.

WINGS GONE BLACK BEAN

☞ **This** recipe was submitted by Salomon Caldeira of Skippers Pub in Northport, New York.

3 tablespoons vegetable oil
20 trimmed and separated
    wings
2 garlic cloves, minced
½ teaspoon chopped fresh
    gingerroot
½ cup chopped green
    onions (scallions)
¼ cup chicken stock

1 tablespoon sweet sherry or
    sake
3 teaspoons soy sauce
1 tablespoon honey
½ teaspoon arrowroot
    starch
¼ cup cooked black beans

1. In a large, heavy skillet or wok, heat the oil over a high flame. Add the wings and fry for 8 minutes, until crispy and brown. Add the garlic, ginger, green onions, chicken stock, sherry, soy sauce, honey, arrowroot, and black beans. Blend with the wings and cook for 5 minutes more, or until heated through.

2. Remove the pan from the heat. Remove the wings with tongs and transfer them to a large mixing bowl. Keep warm.

3. Place the remaining black bean mixture in a blender or food processor. Blend until pureed and smooth. Transfer the sauce with a rubber spatula to the bowl of wings, tossing so they're thoroughly coated.

4. Transfer to a platter and serve with sour cream or blue cheese dressing.

COPACABANA WINGS

☞ **This** recipe was submitted by Salomon Caldeira of Skippers Pub, Northport, New York.

20 trimmed and separated wings
Water, to cover
1 teaspoon crushed dried red pepper
1 teaspoon Tabasco sauce
3 diced plum tomatoes
½ teaspoon ground black pepper

2 teaspoons red wine vinegar
⅓ cup minced onion
3 tablespoons unsalted butter
½ teaspoon salt
⅓ cup chicken stock
½ cup feta cheese

1. Put the wings in a large saucepan and cover with water. Bring to a boil over a high flame, then reduce the heat and simmer for 15 minutes, or until cooked through. Drain the water from the pan while leaving the wings there.

2. Add the crushed pepper, Tabasco, plum tomatoes, black pepper, vinegar, onion, butter, and salt.

3. Turn up the heat again, and sauté all the ingredients in the pan for 5 minutes. Add the chicken stock and simmer for an additional 5 minutes, or until the sauce thickens. Add the feta cheese. Turn off the heat and stir. Add more salt, if needed.

4. Transfer to a platter and serve with rice or mashed potatoes.

DIE-HARD DIJON WINGS

☞ **Another** one from Salomon Caldeira!

¼ cup vegetable oil
20 trimmed and separated
   wings
1 teaspoon minced shallots
1 teaspoon (2 cloves)
   chopped garlic
All-purpose flour, for
   dusting

¼ cup white wine
1 teaspoon crushed dried
   red pepper
1 teaspoon chopped fresh
   parsley
3 tablespoons Dijon mustard
½ cup heavy cream

1. In a large, heavy skillet, heat the oil over a high flame. Add the wings and fry for 5 to 8 minutes, until golden brown. Add the shallots and garlic, and cook for 2 minutes, until lightly brown.

2. Sprinkle flour over the wings and mix well, making sure all the flour is absorbed in the oil. Cook for 2 minutes.

3. Splash in the wine and simmer for 2 minutes. Add the crushed pepper, parsley, mustard, and cream. Simmer for an additional 5 minutes, or until the sauce has lightly coated the wings. Add salt, if needed.

4. Transfer to a platter and serve with crusty French bread.

EMPIRE SWEET 'N' SPICY WINGS

☞ **Rich** Torte, the executive chef at the Inn at Saratoga, submitted this Japanese-inspired recipe. Rich was the 1996 Chef of the Year of the New York Empire State Culinary Association. He has also won various medals from the American Culinary Federation. He can be seen at the Albany, New York, Hot Food Show conducting exciting cooking demonstrations.

2 tablespoons vegetable oil
12 trimmed and separated
  wings
2 thin slices fresh
  gingerroot
2 garlic cloves, minced
2 tablespoons soy sauce

2 teaspoons sambal *(red*
  chile paste)
2 tablespoons light brown
  sugar
1 cup chicken stock
1 tablespoon cornstarch,
  dissolved in ¼ cup water

1. In a large skillet, heat the oil over a high flame. Add the wings and sauté for 5 to 8 minutes, or until brown and crispy. Add the ginger and garlic, browning with the wings for 2 minutes.

2. Add the soy sauce, *sambal,* brown sugar, and chicken stock. Cover the pan with a lid and simmer for 10 minutes. If the sauce hasn't thickened at this point, add a little of the cornstarch mixture, and stir until thickened and glazed.

3. Transfer to a platter and serve with chopsticks and vegetable sushi rolls.

Makes 1 main-dish serving or 2 appetizer servings.

WING CELEBRITIES AND SAUCE MAKERS

Putting this book together gave me the opportunity to meet many great people. I finally got to visit the Anchor Bar in Buffalo, New York! I also went to trade shows, where I met many food and television celebrities, all of whom were excited about this cookbook.

At the Chicago Book Show I met food and fitness guru Richard Simmons—who is, as we all know, a very funny guy. An autographed photo of him hangs in the Anchor Bar, of all places! It says, "Go to health . . . Richard Simmons." He told me he'd be happy to be a part of this book as long as I featured some low-fat recipes. What I like about Richard is that he really does care about people and knows how to motivate them to do their best. Thanks for the encouragement, Richard!

At the Fancy Food Show in New York, I was able to meet the makers of many of the fantastic hot sauces that are on the market. Some of these companies submitted recipes for this book. Some celebrity chefs were present there as well: Tommy Tang, Richard Allen, Larry Forgione, Charlie Trotter, and Paul Prudhomme, who allowed me to print his favorite wing recipes.

Paul is a great guy who is passionate about food and educating America about cooking. He participates in many charity events and always has time to talk to his fans.

Many thanks to everyone who participated in this chapter!

BUFFALO CHICKEN WINGS
BY PAUL PRUDHOMME

24 chicken wings
10 tablespoons (1¼ sticks)
 unsalted butter, divided
1 tablespoon cayenne
 pepper, divided

3 tablespoons Chef Paul
 Prudhomme's Poultry
 Magic, divided
2 cups vegetable oil

1. Remove the chicken wings from the refrigerator and let them come to room temperature. If they're cold, the butter will congeal and won't coat them evenly.

2. Melt 5 tablespoons of the butter with 1½ teaspoons of the cayenne in a small saucepan over medium heat. Remove from the heat and let cool slightly.

3. Cut the chicken wings into three parts at the joints. Discard the tips or use them for another purpose, such as making stock. This will leave two meaty parts per wing for this recipe.

4. Place the wing pieces in a medium mixing bowl, sprinkle with 2 tablespoons of the Poultry Magic, and add the butter-cayenne mixture. Work the butter and seasonings into the wing pieces, distributing as evenly as possible.

5. Heat the oil in a large skillet over high heat to 375° F, using a cooking thermometer or an electric skillet to be sure the oil's temperature is maintained. When the oil reaches 375° F, add as many wing pieces as will fit easily in a single layer. Fry until they're brown, about 4 to 6 minutes. Drain on paper towels and repeat with the remaining chicken.

6. Meanwhile, melt the remaining 5 tablespoons of butter in a small skillet over low heat. Add the remaining Poultry Magic and cayenne, cook until the butter starts to brown, then remove from the heat. When all the wing pieces are cooked, put them in a bowl and pour the hot seasoned butter over them, then toss until the chicken is coated.

7. Serve immediately with blue cheese dressing, Chef Paul Prudhomme's Magic Pepper Sauce, and celery sticks. Makes 2 large main-dish servings or 4 large appetizer servings.

Chef Paul Prudhomme Magic Seasoning Blend®;
Pure Magic Cookbook © 1995;
special thanks to the McBride family.

BROILED HONEY WINGS BY PAUL PRUDHOMME

8 chicken wings
2 tablespoons Paul Prudhomme's Meat Magic
1½ teaspoons ground ginger
1 teaspoon ground California Beauty chile pepper
½ teaspoon rubbed sage
¼ teaspoon ground cumin

¼ cup (½ stick) unsalted butter
½ cup chopped onion
2 teaspoons minced fresh garlic
½ cup dry sherry
2 tablespoons soy sauce
½ cup chicken stock
½ cup honey

1. If you're using an electric broiler, preheat.

2. Cut the chicken wings into three parts at the joints. Discard the tips, or reserve them for making stock. This will leave two meaty parts per wing. Combine the Meat Magic, ginger, chile, sage, and cumin in a small bowl. Sprinkle 1 tablespoon of this seasoning mix over the wings and rub it in well.

3. Melt the butter in a heavy 12-inch skillet over high heat. When the butter sizzles, add the wing pieces and brown them on one side. Turn them over, add the onion and garlic, and cook, occasionally scraping the pan, until the chicken is browned on the other side, about 10 to 12 minutes in all.

4. Add the sherry, soy sauce, stock, and the remaining seasoning mix, stir, and bring to a full boil. Remove from the heat, add the honey, and let sit for 3 minutes.

5. If you're using a gas broiler, turn it on. With tongs, remove the wings from the sauce and place them under the broiler in a single layer. Broil, turning once, until they're browned and crisp, about 2 minutes on each side. Pour the sauce into a bowl for dipping, and serve with the wings immediately. Makes two appetizer servings.

Chef Paul Prudhomme Magic Seasoning Blend®;
Pure Magic Cookbook © 1995;
special thanks to the McBride family.

TAHITI JOE POLYNESIAN WING PIZZA

☞ **Tahiti Joe** makes awesome, distinctive hot sauces like the one in this recipe.

4 ounces boneless chicken
   tenders
4 tablespoons Tahiti Joe
   Polynesian Hot
   Sauce

2 tablespoons diced,
   drained canned
   pineapple
1 small (12-inch) frozen
   ready-bake pizza

1. Preheat the oven to 350° F.

2. Cut the chicken tenders into bite-sized pieces. Place in a lightly oiled skillet over a high flame. Add the hot sauce. Reduce the heat, stir in the chicken, and cook the chicken in the hot sauce over very low heat for 10 to 12 minutes, until all liquid is absorbed and the chicken is glazed.

3. Remove the chicken from the pan, and transfer to the frozen pizza. Spread the chicken evenly over the pizza and top with the pineapple.

4. Place the frozen pizza on a lightly greased baking sheet and bake for 10 minutes, or until crispy.

Makes 2 to 4 servings.

Recipe submitted by Tahiti Joe Hot Sauces, West Palm Beach, Florida.

WRONG NUMBER!
HOT CRISPY WINGS

☞ **This** recipe was submitted by Peppergirl sauces, known for their exotic-looking and -tasting hot sauce.

¼ cup olive oil
2 (5-ounce) bottles
* Peppergirl Wrong*
* Number Chipotle*
* Habañero Hot Sauce*

30 wing drummettes, with
* the skin removed*
Fifi's Nasty Little Secret
* Dipping Sauce*
* (see page 142)*

1. Preheat the oven to 325° F.

2. In a medium bowl, whisk the olive oil with the hot sauce. Set aside.

3. Arrange the drummettes on an olive-oil rubbed shallow baking pan and bake for 25 minutes.

4. Remove the wings from the pan, and preheat the broiler. Transfer the wings to the bowl with the sauce mixture, coating them thoroughly.

5. Transfer the sauce-saturated wings back to the baking pan and place under the broiler for 5 minutes, or until brown and crispy.

6. Transfer to a platter and serve with Fifi's Nasty Little Secret Dipping Sauce.

Makes 2 to 4 entree servings or 4 to 6 appetizer servings.

FIFI'S NASTY LITTLE SECRET DIPPING SAUCE

1 pint low-fat sour cream
1 (5-ounce) bottle
   Peppergirl Nasty Little
   Secret Pineapple
   Jalapeño Hot Sauce

½ cup applesauce

In a small mixing bowl, combine the sour cream, hot sauce, and applesauce. Blend until smooth and serve immediately with Wrong Number Wings.

Recipes submitted by
Peppergirl Sauces, Van Nuys, California.

SPICY PECAN BATTERED CHICKEN WINGS

24 trimmed and separated
chicken wings
1 cup Crystal Wing Sauce
1 cup roasted hot pepper
pecans (recipe follows)
1 cup all-purpose flour
1 cup yellow cornmeal
1 teaspoon salt

1 tablespoon ground black
pepper
1 tablespoon cayenne
pepper
3 large eggs, beaten
1 cup whole milk
Vegetable oil, for frying

1. Combine the wings and hot sauce in a plastic container, coating the wings thoroughly. Cover and refrigerate for 4 hours, stirring occasionally.

2. Prepare the roasted pecans (see below). Cool the pecans to room temperature and grind them in a food processor or coffee grinder until they resemble coarsely ground cornmeal.

3. In a large mixing bowl, combine the ground pecans, flour, cornmeal, salt, pepper, and cayenne; mix well.

4. In a separate, medium mixing bowl, whisk the eggs and milk.

5. Remove the wings from the marinade and dip in the egg mixture, making sure they're thoroughly coated.

6. Press and roll the wings in the dry mixture, coating them on all sides.

7. Heat 2 inches of oil in a large, heavy skillet over a hot flame, or heat the oil in a fryer to 350° F. Fry the wings one at a time for 5 to 8 minutes, or until they start to float and are a deep walnut color. Serve with a side of hot sauce.

Makes 2 entree servings or 4 to 6 appetizer servings.

Recipe submitted by
Crystal Hot Sauce, New Orleans, Louisiana.

ROASTED HOT PEPPER PECANS

¼ pound (1 stick) unsalted butter
4 cups chopped pecans
4 tablespoons Crystal Worcestershire sauce

4 tablespoons Crystal Hot Sauce
Salt to taste

1. Melt the butter in a heavy frying pan over medium heat and sauté the pecans, being careful not to burn them.

2. Add the Worcestershire and hot sauces several drops at a time until it is well distributed. When all liquid is absorbed, remove the pecans from the heat and sprinkle with salt to taste.

SPICY CHICKEN WINGS

☞ **Chef** Roy M. Leinfuss from Eat This, Inc., sent me this recipe to use with their "soulful" hot sauces.

¼ cup vegetable oil

20 trimmed and separated
   wings

1 cup soy sauce

⅔ cup olive oil

4 teaspoons finely chopped
   fresh rosemary

1 teaspoon garlic powder

2 teaspoons fresh lemon
   juice

⅔ teaspoon cayenne pepper

4 dashes Worcestershire
   sauce

6–8 dashes hot sauce

1. In a large, heavy skillet, heat the oil over a high flame. Add the wings and fry for 10 to 12 minutes, or until brown, crispy, and cooked through. Remove from the heat and set aside.

2. In a large mixing bowl, whisk the soy sauce, oil, rosemary, garlic powder, lemon juice, cayenne, Worcestershire, and hot sauce.

3. Add the cooked wings, coating them thoroughly.

4. Transfer to a platter, and serve with blue cheese dip and celery sticks. For a unique variation, try this wing recipe with Eat This, Inc.'s, Strawberry Habañero Soul Sauce. Just toss the wings with the sauce!

Recipes submitted by
Eat This, Inc., Breckenridge, Colorado.

WING PARTY RECIPES

f you're planning a wingfest (for the Super Bowl, for example), here are some helpful hints and recipes.

PARTY PLANNING

Careful planning is the key to success, because it will guarantee peace of mind for the host. (Don't you want to enjoy the party, too?)

Write down your party ideas early. This will allow you to do and buy the most important things first. Evaluate all the factors involved in having this party: the date, the place, the budget you'll be working with. Will your party have a theme? Will there be music? Will you need to rent anything (chairs, tables, a Chicken Wing Orchestra)? Will you send out invitations? (If you do, make sure they go out at least two weeks before the party.)

MENU

Some like their wings hot . . . and some don't. Make sure you have sauces with various levels of heat available at the table—and label them so no one gets confused! In the chapter "Dips, Salads, and Side Dishes," you'll find recipes for dishes to serve with the wings; coleslaw, potato, and macaroni salads are always favorites. Put out plates of carrot and celery sticks, blue cheese dip, and don't forget—plenty of water and other beverages to drink, and plenty of napkins to wipe up with!

Final note: Unless otherwise noted, the recipes in this chapter are designed to serve a large group of people: fifteen to twenty people as an entree and forty to fifty people as an appetizer.

ORIGINAL BUFFALO PARTY WINGS

☞ **This** simple recipe is the one that made wings famous. It's an all-time favorite with everybody. These wings should go over well at your party!

2 cups (1 pound) hot, melted, clarified unsalted butter

3 cups Frank's REDHOT Cayenne Pepper Sauce

20 pounds (around 200) trimmed and separated wings

Vegetable oil, for frying

1. Combine the hot, clarified butter and hot sauce in a large bowl. Mix well. Keep warm.

2. Heat the oil in a fryer to 350° F and deep-fry the chicken wings for 12 to 14 minutes, or until crispy, brown, and cooked through. Drain well.

3. Add the wings to the sauce and toss well to coat. Keep warm.

4. Serve with blue cheese dip and celery sticks.

Recipe submitted by Reckitt & Coleman
Commercial Group, Springfield, Missouri.

FEATHERWEIGHT PARTY WINGS

☞ **If** your guests crave a healthier alternative, these wings are an ideal choice—a lean and mean version of the original.

2 tablespoons cornstarch
2 cups cold chicken broth
3 cups Frank's Original
   REDHOT Sauce

¼ cup vegetable oil
20 pounds (around 200)
   trimmed and separated
   wings

1. In a medium saucepan over high heat, combine the cold chicken stock and cornstarch, whisking well. Bring to a boil while stirring in the hot sauce and oil.

2. Simmer for 3 minutes. Remove from the heat and set aside to cool for 10 minutes. Add the wings, coating them thoroughly. Marinate in the refrigerator for 2 hours.

3. Preheat the oven to 400° F. Spray or brush four large baking sheets with oil. Spread the wings evenly on the sheets, and bake for 30 minutes. If you prefer them very crispy, turn the wings and bake an additional 10 to 15 minutes.

© Reckitt & Coleman

GOLD FEVER PARTY WINGS

☞ **This** is a kinder, gentler version of America's favorite appetizer. This version would also appeal to the younger ones in your party—kind of a training version for the kids.

2½ cups Original REDHOT Cayenne pepper sauce
2½ cups Cattlemen's Gold Sweet & Tangy Sauce

Vegetable oil, for frying
20 pounds (around 200) trimmed and separated wings

1. Combine the hot sauce and Cattlemen's Gold Sauce in a large mixing bowl. Mix well and set aside.

2. Heat the oil in a fryer to 350° F and deep-fry the wings for 12 to 14 minutes, or until crispy brown and cooked through. Drain well.

3. Add the wings to the sauce, coating them thoroughly. Keep warm.

4. Serve with blue cheese dip and celery sticks.

© Reckitt & Coleman

WESTERN PARTY WINGS

☞ **Your** guests will go wild over this western variation on the wing theme. These tangy, saucy wings have a distinctively western barbecue flavor with a hint of garlic. Serve 'em up and move 'em out!

¼ cup Original REDHOT
  sauce
4 cups Cattlemen's Original
  Barbecue Sauce
½ cup French's Dijon
  mustard
3 tablespoons garlic powder
Vegetable oil, for frying
20 pounds (around 200)
  trimmed and separated
  wings

1. Combine the hot sauce, barbecue sauce, mustard, and garlic powder in a medium saucepan. Simmer for 4 to 5 minutes, then remove them from heat and transfer to a large mixing bowl. Keep warm.

2. Heat the oil in a fryer to 350° F and deep-fry the wings for 12 to 14 minutes, or until crispy brown and cooked through. Drain well.

3. Add the wings to the sauce and toss to coat. Keep warm.

4. Serve with blue cheese dip and celery sticks.

© Reckitt & Coleman

HONEY-MUSTARD PARTY WINGS

☞ **Honey** mustard is a magic maker—everybody loves the combination of sweet and pungent. These are good wings to have as a second choice at your party.

1½ cups Frank's Original
  REDHOT Cayenne Pepper
  sauce
2 cups French's Dijon
  mustard
3 cups honey
Vegetable oil, for frying
20 pounds (around 200)
  trimmed and separated
  wings

1. Combine the hot sauce, mustard, and honey in a medium saucepan. Stir over medium heat for 2 to 3 minutes, or until the honey is blended. Remove from the heat and transfer to a large mixing bowl. Keep warm.

2. Heat the oil in a fryer to 350° F and deep-fry the wings for 12 to 14 minutes, or until crispy brown and cooked through. Drain well.

3. Add the wings to the sauce and toss to coat. Keep warm.

4. Serve with blue cheese dip and celery sticks.

© Reckitt & Coleman

SHANGHAI RED WINGS

Vegetable oil, for frying
2½ pounds (around 25)
   trimmed and separated
   wings
¼ cup soy sauce
3 tablespoons honey
3 tablespoons REDHOT
   sauce

2 tablespoons peanut oil
1 teaspoon grated fresh
   gingerroot
1 teaspoon (2 cloves)
   minced fresh garlic

1. Heat the oil in a fryer to 400° F and deep-fry the wings for 12 minutes, or until crispy and no longer pink; drain well.

2. Combine the soy sauce, honey, hot sauce, peanut oil, ginger, and garlic in a small bowl. Mix well.

3. Pour the sauce over the fried wings and toss to coat.

Makes 4 to 6 appetizer servings or 2 entree servings.

© Reckitt & Coleman

CAJUN WINGS

Vegetable oil, for frying
2½ pounds (around 25)
   trimmed and separated
   wings
⅓ cup Frank's REDHOT
   Sauce

⅓ cup ketchup
¼ cup (¼ stick) melted
   butter or margarine
2 teaspoons Cajun
   seasoning

1. Heat the oil in a fryer to 400° F and deep-fry the wings for 12 minutes, or until crispy and no longer pink; drain well.

2. Combine the hot sauce, ketchup, butter, and Cajun seasoning in a small bowl. Mix well.

3. Pour the sauce over the wings and toss to coat.

Makes 4 to 6 appetizer servings or 2 entree servings.

© *Reckitt & Coleman*

SANTE FE WINGS

Vegetable oil, for frying
2½ pounds (around 25)
   trimmed and separated
   wings
¼ cup (½ stick) hot, melted
   unsalted butter or
   margarine

¼ cup Frank's Original
   REDHOT Sauce
¼ cup chile sauce
1 teaspoon chile powder

153

1. Heat the oil in a fryer to 400° F and deep-fry the wings for 12 minutes, or until crispy and no longer pink; drain well.

2. Combine the melted butter, hot sauce, chile sauce, and chile powder in a small bowl. Mix well.

3. Pour the sauce over the wings and toss to coat.

Makes 4 to 6 appetizer servings or 2 entree servings.

© Reckitt & Coleman

SWEET 'N' SPICY WINGS

Vegetable oil, for frying
2½ pounds (around 25)
   trimmed and separated
   wings
⅓ cup Frank's REDHOT
   Sauce
¼ cup (½ stick) butter

2 tablespoons thawed frozen
   orange juice concentrate
2 tablespoons honey
¼ teaspoon ground
   cinnamon
¼ teaspoon ground allspice

1. Heat the oil in a fryer to 400° F and deep-fry the wings for 12 minutes, or until crispy and no longer pink; drain well.

2. Combine the hot sauce, butter, orange juice, honey, cinnamon, and allspice in a small, microwavable bowl. Microwave on high for 1 minute, or until the butter is melted. Stir until smooth.

3. Pour the sauce over the wings, and toss to coat.

Makes 4 to 6 appetizer servings or 2 entree servings.

© Reckitt & Coleman

KENTUCKY-STYLE WINGS

Vegetable oil, for frying
2½ pounds (around 25)
   trimmed and separated
   wings
¼ cup (½ stick) hot, melted
   unsalted butter or
   margarine

¼ cup Frank's REDHOT
   sauce
2 tablespoons pancake
   syrup
2 tablespoons bourbon

1. Heat the oil in a fryer to 400° F and deep-fry the wings for 12 minutes, or until crispy and no longer pink; drain well.

2. Combine the butter, hot sauce, syrup, and bourbon in a large bowl. Mix well.

3. Pour the sauce over the wings, and toss to coat.

Makes 4 to 6 appetizer servings or 2 entree servings.

© *Reckitt & Coleman*

BUFFALO BAR-B-Q NUGGETS

☞ **Here's** a version of the boneless wing.

½ cup Frank's Original
REDHOT Cayenne Pepper
Sauce
⅓ cup (⅔ stick) hot, melted
unsalted butter
1½ pounds boneless,
skinless chicken breasts
or thighs

Lettuce leaves
Blue cheese salad dressing
(optional)

1. Combine the hot sauce and butter in a small mixing bowl; mix well. Reserve 1/3 cup of this sauce mixture, and pour the remainder over the chicken. Cover and refrigerate for 20 minutes.

2. Oil a grill or barbecue, and bring it to medium heat. Place the chicken pieces on it, discarding any remaining marinade. Grill for about 10 minutes, or until no longer pink in the center.

3. In a small saucepan, heat the reserved sauce. Cut the cooked chicken into bite-sized pieces and mix these into the warmed sauce.

4. Arrange the chicken on a lettuce-lined platter. Serve with blue cheese dressing, if desired.

Makes 4 to 6 appetizer servings or 2 entree servings.

© *Reckitt & Coleman*

HOMEMADE WINGS

This chapter features recipes from "regular people" who love wings and have created recipes in their home kitchens.

Cooking at home, rather than in a commercial kitchen, forces us to be creative. Standard kitchens just don't have the powerful equipment or supplies available in restaurants. So we experiment with different recipes by using whatever we have on hand in the pantry.

Cooking at home also allows us to work with our families. When I was a child, for instance, I would do the prep work in the kitchen for my mother. She got home around six in the evening and needed only to put the finishing touches on the meal. We had a delicious, healthy, home-cooked dinner every night. Perhaps you can work out a similar system with your partner or children.

Final note: I know wings are not always 100 percent nutritious—but all of us need to be "bad" once in a while!

MARGARITA ON THE WINGS

☞ **Pam** and Pete are famous for their Caribbean-style house parties, at which all the guests have instruments or drums pushed into their hands so they can contribute to the craziness. Their wings are perfect for the exhausted orchestra leader and his bandmates.

2 tablespoons vegetable oil
20 trimmed and separated
   wings
1/4 cup tequila
1/2 teaspoon salt
1/2 teaspoon black pepper
1/2 teaspoon onion powder
Dash hot sauce

2/3 cup bottled margarita
   mix
1 teaspoon grated
   horseradish
2 tablespoons (1/4 stick)
   unsalted butter
Juice of 1/2 lime

1. In a large, heavy skillet, heat the oil over a high flame. Add the wings and fry for 5 to 8 minutes, or until crispy and brown.

2. Carefully add the tequila. Ignite, if you wish, or let simmer for 5 minutes, until the alcohol has burned off.

3. Sprinkle the salt, pepper, and onion powder over wings. Stir to seal in their flavor. Add the hot sauce and let it blend in for 2 minutes.

4. Add the margarita mix, horseradish, butter, and lime juice. Reduce the heat and let the wings slowly simmer for 5 minutes, or until the sauce sticks to them like a glaze.

5. Transfer to a platter, garnish with fresh lime slices, and bring out the band.

Recipe by Pam and Pete Marino, Huntington, New York.

BABA BOOEY'S FUNKY MONKEY WINGS

☞ **This** recipe is great for parties, and bananas are healthful and rich in potassium. If you're still skeptical about these wings, just wait till you try them.

2 tablespoons vegetable oil
20 trimmed and separated
 wings
1 ripe banana, sliced
¼ cup dark rum
1 tablespoon light brown
 sugar
½ teaspoon dried ginger
½ teaspoon ground
 cinnamon

½ teaspoon salt
¼ cup (½ stick) unsalted
 butter
2 tablespoons hot sauce
¼ cup heavy cream
¼ cup water
Juice of ½ lime
Water, for steaming

1. In a large, heavy skillet, heat the oil over a high flame. Add the wings and fry for 10 to 12 minutes, or until brown and cooked through. Turn off the heat and remove the wings; set them aside.

2. Turn the heat to high again. In the same skillet, brown the sliced banana. Carefully add the rum and ignite if you wish, or let simmer for 3 minutes until the alcohol has burned off.

3. Add the brown sugar and stir until the banana becomes pasty. Lower the heat and add the ginger, cinnamon, salt, butter, and hot sauce.

4. Remove the pan from the heat and transfer the banana mixture to a blender or food processor. Puree, while slowly adding the cream, ¼ cup water, and lime juice, until smooth, then set aside.

5. Clean the skillet and return it to the stove over a high flame. Toss the cooked wings in the pan with ¼ cup of water to steam and reheat the wings.

6. Add the pureed banana mixture to the wings. Once the sauce starts sticking to the wings, remove them from the heat.

7. Transfer to a platter, garnish with strawberries, and do the "Funky Monkey!"

Recipe by Pam and Pete Marino, Huntington, New York.

BRATEN WINGS

☞ **Brían** Roesch of East Northport, New York, created this great wing recipe using the German sauerbraten technique. These wings go down great with some Bavarian brewskies . . . Prosit!

2 quarts water
2 cups red wine vinegar
½ cup pickling spice
2 medium onions, minced
20 trimmed and separated
   wings

¼ cup (½ stick) unsalted
   butter
4 teaspoons light brown
   sugar
½ teaspoon salt

1. If you're broiling the wings, preheat the broiler.

2. Bring the water, vinegar, pickling spice and onions to a boil in a medium saucepan. Add the wings and simmer for 30 minutes. Remove the wings and set aside.

3. Make a glaze for the wings by melting the butter in a small saucepan over a low flame. Stir in the brown sugar. Remove the pan from the heat once the sugar has dissolved.

4. Spread the wings on a buttered baking pan and place in the broiler or on a medium-heat barbecue or grill.

5. Brush the wings with the brown sugar glaze, and cook for 5 minutes, until wings are pleasantly glazed and brown.

DENISE'S FAMOUS ZESTY WINGS

☞ **Deníse** works for the Alliant/Kraft food service in New Jersey. She heard through the grapevine that I was looking for wing recipes. She was happy to share this one with us!

20 trimmed and separated wings

1 cup bottled Italian dressing

2 tablespoons (¼ stick) melted unsalted butter

¼ cup hot sauce

½ cup barbecue sauce

1 tablespoon dark chile powder

½ teaspoon cayenne pepper

1. Preheat the oven to 350° F.

2. In a large bowl, combine the wings with the Italian dressing. Marinate in the refrigerator for 6 hours. Drain, discarding the excess marinade.

3. In a large mixing bowl, combine the melted butter, hot sauce, barbecue sauce, chile powder, and cayenne. Mix well. Add the wings, coating them thoroughly.

4. Transfer the wings with tongs to a buttered 2-inch-deep baking dish and bake for 25 to 30 minutes, turning occasionally, until glazed and cooked through.

5. To achieve more crispiness, carefully drain the excess liquid from the pan and place the wings under the broiler for 5 minutes.

6. Transfer to a platter, and serve with blue cheese dip and celery sticks.

Recipe by Denise Bartone, New Jersey.

MOM MILLER'S SWEET 'N' SOUR WINGS

☞ **Mom** Miller is one of my most loyal cooking students—she's been studying with me for five years. I have nominated her for class president because this charming, adorable lady maintains order in my class with an iron fist. Raising the rolling pin is her favorite technique when there's too much yapping going on.

1 (16-ounce) can crushed
    pineapple
1 tablespoon cornstarch
⅓ cup sugar
¼ cup soy sauce
2 tablespoons white vinegar

1 garlic clove, minced
¼ teaspoon dried ginger
¼ teaspoon ground black
    pepper
20 trimmed and separated
    wings

1. Preheat the oven to 350° F.

2. In a small saucepan over a high flame, drain the juice from the pineapple can. Reserve the pineapple. Whisk in the cornstarch quickly, before juice gets hot. Add the sugar, soy sauce, vinegar, garlic, ginger, and pepper.

3. Bring the mixture to a bubbling simmer. Add the crushed pineapple and simmer for 2 minutes. Remove from the heat, and let cool for 10 minutes. Transfer to a large bowl.

4. Add the wings to the pineapple mixture, coating them thoroughly.

5. Spread the wings evenly on a buttered 2-inch-deep baking dish. Bake for 20 to 25 minutes, or until thickly coated, glazed, and cooked through.

6. Transfer the wings to a platter garnished with red cocktail cherries.

Recipe by Eleanor "Mom" Miller, Smithtown, New York.

FULLER BUFFALO WINGS

☞ ❙ received this recipe from my editor, Lynda Dickey, and her friend Becky, who are fans of Buffalo wings. During the production of this book I sent them Buffalo wings from the Anchor Bar in Buffalo, New York, to get them through until the book was published. Thanks for your patience!

*½ cup hot sauce
(not Tabasco)
2¼ teaspoons white vinegar
1 tablespoon unsalted butter*

*20 trimmed and separated
wings
½ (1.2-ounces) package
ranch dressing mix*

1. Preheat the oven to 350° F.

2. In a small saucepan over a low flame, heat the hot sauce, vinegar, and butter until melted. Transfer to a large mixing bowl. Let cool for 20 minutes.

3. Add the wings to the sauce mixture, coating them thoroughly.

4. Spread the wings evenly on a buttered 2-inch-deep baking dish. Sprinkle evenly with the ranch dressing mix.

5. Bake for 25 to 30 minutes, occasionally turning and basting with the sauce remaining in the bowl.

6. Transfer to a platter and serve with blue cheese dressing, celery, and carrot sticks.

Recipe by Becky Fuller, Connecticut.

JAMAICA JAMAICA WINGS

☞ **Jamaican** and West Indian cooking is big time in Jamaica, Queens, New York. On every street corner you can buy or eat this cuisine. I never fail to stop by for a bite of roti or jerk chicken when I happen to be in the vicinity. Darryl got this recipe from his mother.

1 cup (½ pound, or 2 sticks) unsalted butter, melted

½ cup tomato juice

½ cup Jamaican jerk seasoning

½ tablespoon hot sauce

1 tablespoon dark Jamaican rum

Vegetable oil, for frying

20 trimmed and separated wings

All-purpose flour, for dusting

1. In a large mixing bowl, combine the butter, tomato juice, seasoning, hot sauce, and rum. Mix well and set aside.

2. In a large, heavy skillet, heat 2 inches of oil over a high flame.

3. Dust the wings with flour, making sure they're thoroughly coated.

4. Drop the wings into the oil and fry for 10 to 12 minutes, or until golden brown, crispy, and cooked through. Drain well.

5. Add the wings to the sauce and toss, making sure they're thoroughly coated.

6. Turn on some reggae music and have a Wing Jam!

Recipe by Darryl Brooks, Jamaica, New York.

MR. COLA WINGS

☞ **Wings** go better with . . . Coke!

1 cup cola
1 cup ketchup
¼ cup (½ stick) unsalted
   butter, melted
1 teaspoon hot sauce
¼ teaspoon ground black
   pepper

1 tablespoon dark brown
   sugar
20 trimmed and separated
   wings

1. Combine the cola, ketchup, butter, hot sauce, pepper, and brown sugar in a small saucepan over medium heat. When sauce is warm and the sugar is dissolved, remove from heat and cool.

2. Place the wings in the cooled sauce and marinate in the refrigerator for 2 hours.

3. Preheat the oven to 350° F. Spread the wings evenly on a greased baking sheet and bake for 30 minutes, turning and basting wings after 15 minutes.

Recipe submitted by Debra Cotter, Camden, New Jersey.

RED, RED WINE WINGS

☞ **This** is a Swedish-influenced wing recipe. Lingonberry jelly is available at most gourmet shops, or at Ikea. There is more to Swedish food than gravlax and Swedish meatballs!

3 tablespoons soy sauce
3 tablespoons fresh orange juice
5 tablespoons sweet red wine
1 tablespoon minced fresh gingerroot
1 garlic clove, minced
3 tablespoons red lingonberry jelly

1 tablespoon light brown sugar
⅛ teaspoon ground cloves
⅛ teaspoon ground cardamom
1 tablespoon orange zest (use a zester)
20 trimmed and separated wings

1. In a small saucepan over a high flame, combine the soy sauce, orange juice, wine, ginger, garlic, jelly, brown sugar, cloves, cardamom, and orange zest. Stir and bring to a boil, then lower the heat and simmer for 3 minutes. Remove from the heat and let cool for 20 minutes.

2. Place the wings on a medium-heat grill or barbecue. Brush them generously with the prepared glaze. Continue to glaze and turn the wings for 25 to 30 minutes, or until brown, glazed, and cooked through.

3. Transfer to a platter and have a Swedish Midsummer Fest.

Recipe by Carl Larson, Daytona, Florida.

PARMI WINGS

☞ **Everybody** loves chicken Parmesan; why not wings Parmesan? Dave reminds us to use clean, fresh oil for best results.

¼ cup all-purpose flour
⅛ teaspoon salt
⅛ teaspoon ground black
   pepper
⅛ teaspoon garlic powder
20 trimmed and separated
   wings

3 large eggs
½ cup grated Parmesan
   cheese
½ cup bread crumbs
¼ teaspoon dried basil
¼ teaspoon dried oregano
Vegetable oil, for frying

1. In a large mixing bowl, combine the flour, salt, pepper, and garlic powder. Add the wings, coating them thoroughly.

2. In a separate, medium bowl, beat the eggs. Set aside.

3. In another medium bowl, combine the Parmesan, bread crumbs, basil, and oregano.

4. Dip the floured wings one at a time into the egg mixture, then press each wing into the bread crumb mixture. Place all the breaded wings onto a baking sheet and freeze for 1 hour. This will firm the breading and create a better crust when frying.

5. Heat the oil in a deep-fryer to 350° F. Fry the wings for 5 minutes, until golden brown, crispy, and cooked through. If the wings are still pink inside, place them in a 325° F oven for an additional 5 to 8 minutes.

6. Serve with marinara sauce and garlic bread.

Recipe by Dave Leonard, San Diego, California.

CITRUS-ROSEMARY WINGS

☞ **If** you think lemonade is only a thirst quencher, look what it does to these wings!

¼ cup olive oil
¼ cup (½ stick) unsalted
  butter, melted
¼ cup minced fresh shallots
1 tablespoons (5 cloves)
  minced fresh garlic
1 tablespoon chopped fresh
  rosemary

½ cup fresh orange juice
½ cup lemonade
Dash each salt, pepper, and
  hot sauce
20 trimmed and separated
  wings

1. In a large mixing bowl, combine the oil, butter, shallots, garlic, rosemary, orange juice, lemonade, pepper, salt, and hot sauce. Mix until smooth.

2. Add the wings, coating them thoroughly. Marinate in the refrigerator for 4 hours to develop their flavor.

3. Place the wings on a medium-heat grill or barbecue, occasionally turning and basting, for 25 to 30 minutes, until brown and cooked through. Enjoy with lemonade!

Recipe by Mark McDermott, Rockford, Illinois.

WING BUTTERS

ere, as a special bonus, are six more ways to pre-pare wings! If you like wings with butter alone or want to enhance your favorite sauce, use one of these wing butters. They're all simple to make and use: Prepare them in advance and store them in rolls in your freezer, kind of like premade cookie dough. When you want extra flavor, just grill, bake, or fry some wings as usual. Leave them plain or toss them with some hot sauce in a bowl. Then just slice a few thin pieces of wing butter from the roll in your freezer and toss with the wings while they're still warm. That's it! You can reseal the ends of the roll and put it back in the freezer to use next time.

WICKED BLUE CHEESE BUTTER

*1 cup (½ pound, or 2 sticks)
    softened unsalted butter
⅔ cup crumbled blue cheese
⅔ cup chopped fresh parsley
¼ cup brandy*

*2 garlic cloves, minced
⅛ teaspoon onion powder
⅛ teaspoon ground black
    pepper
⅛ teaspoon hot sauce*

1. In a medium bowl, cream together the butter, blue cheese, parsley, brandy, garlic, onion powder, pepper, and hot sauce.

2. With a rubber spatula, place the mixture widthwise down the middle of a 12 × 8-inch sheet of tinfoil or wax paper, leaving about an inch free at either end. Roll the foil or paper up lengthwise to create a little cylinder of butter. Seal the ends of the cylinder and freeze for at least 1 hour before using.

BAD BREATH BUTTER

1 cup (½ pound, or 2 sticks) softened unsalted butter	¼ teaspoon ground black pepper
1 cup chopped fresh basil	¼ teaspoon onion powder
6 garlic cloves, minced	¼ teaspoon cayenne pepper

1. In a medium bowl, cream together the butter, basil, garlic, pepper, onion powder, and cayenne.

2. With a rubber spatula, place the mixture widthwise down the middle of a 12 × 8-inch sheet of tinfoil or wax paper, leaving about an inch free at either end. Roll the foil or paper up lengthwise to create a little cylinder of butter. Seal the ends of the cylinder and freeze for at least 1 hour before using.

HELL-BENT FOR GORGONZOLA BUTTER

1 cup (½ pound, or 2 sticks)
    softened unsalted butter
⅓ cup crumbled Gorgonzola
    cheese
¼ cup chopped fresh parsley
1 teaspoon cracked black
    pepper

¼ teaspoon cayenne pepper
¼ teaspoon onion powder
¼ teaspoon garlic powder
Dash hot sauce

1. In a medium bowl, cream together the butter, cheese, parsley, pepper, cayenne, onion and garlic powders, and hot sauce.

2. With a rubber spatula, place the mixture widthwise down the middle of a 12 × 8-inch sheet of tinfoil or wax paper, leaving about an inch free at either end. Roll the foil or paper up lengthwise to create a little cylinder of butter. Seal the ends of the cylinder and freeze for at least 1 hour before using.

ZESTY BUTTER

1 cup (½ pound, or 2 sticks)
    softened unsalted butter
½ teaspoon lime zest (use a
    zester)
1 tablespoon fresh lime juice
½ teaspoon lemon zest (use
    a zester)

1 tablespoon fresh lemon
    juice
1 tablespoon chopped fresh
    cilantro
½ teaspoon crushed dried
    red pepper

1. In a medium mixing bowl, cream together the butter, lime zest and juice, lemon zest and juice, cilantro, and crushed pepper.

2. With a rubber spatula, place the mixture widthwise down the middle of a 12 × 8-inch sheet of tinfoil or wax paper, leaving about an inch free at either end. Roll the foil or paper up lengthwise to create a little cylinder of butter. Seal the ends of the cylinder and freeze for at least 1 hour before using.

DIJON BUTTER

*1 cup (½ pound, or 2 sticks)
  softened unsalted butter*
¼ cup Dijon mustard
2 large shallots, minced
*1 teaspoon cracked black
  pepper*

½ cup chopped fresh parsley
¼ teaspoon onion powder
*¼ teaspoon crushed dried
  red pepper*
Dash hot sauce

1. In a medium mixing bowl, cream together the butter, mustard, shallots, black pepper, parsley, onion powder, crushed pepper, and hot sauce.

2. With a rubber spatula, place the mixture widthwise down the middle of a 12 × 8-inch sheet of tinfoil or wax paper, leaving about an inch free at either end. Roll the foil or paper up lengthwise to create a little cylinder of butter. Seal the ends of the cylinder and freeze for at least 1 hour before using.

BLIMEY LIMEY BUTTER

1 cup (½ pound, or 2 sticks)
  softened unsalted butter
4 teaspoons fresh lime juice
1 tablespoon lime zest (use
  a zester)

1 tablespoon soy sauce
1 tablespoon teriyaki sauce
½ teaspoon crushed dried
  red pepper

1. In a medium bowl, cream together the butter, lime juice and zest, soy sauce, teriyaki sauce, and crushed pepper.

2. With a rubber spatula, place the mixture widthwise down the middle of a 12 × 8-inch sheet of tinfoil or wax paper, leaving about an inch free at either end. Roll the foil or paper up lengthwise to create a little cylinder of butter. Seal the ends of the cylinder and freeze for at least 1 hour before using.

DIPS, SALADS, AND SIDE DISHES

Wings can be so much more than appetizers. When served with a salad and a side dish, you have a delicious, hearty meal! In the following chapter, you will find delicious dips, cold salads, and hot side dishes that make great accompaniments to wings.

Please note that many of the recipes are spicy. If that creates a problem for you, your kids, or any of your guests, just leave out or reduce the spice or hot sauce. Whoever wants to can add extra later onto his or her own serving.

DIPS

ROQUEFORT DIP

☞ **This** dip is great with hot wings and celery and carrot sticks.

1 cup sour cream
¼ cup buttermilk
¼ cup mayonnaise
1 garlic clove, minced

1 tablespoon Dijon mustard
½ cup crumbled Roquefort
  cheese

1. In a medium mixing bowl, combine the sour cream, buttermilk, mayonnaise, garlic, mustard, and Roquefort. Mix well.

2. Chill in the refrigerator before serving.

Makes 2 cups.

JALAPEÑO DIP

☞ **This** is a special dip for milder wings, to create a spicy contrast.

1 cup sour cream
½ cup mayonnaise
2 garlic cloves, minced
1 jalapeño pepper, seeded
   and minced
3 tablespoons chopped fresh
   cilantro

½ teaspoon ground cumin
½ teaspoon onion powder
⅛ teaspoon salt
⅛ teaspoon ground black
   pepper

1. In a medium mixing bowl, combine the sour cream, mayonnaise, garlic, jalapeño, cilantro, cumin, onion powder, salt, and pepper. Mix well.

2. Chill in the refrigerator before serving.

Makes 2 cups.

CILANTRO DIP

☞ **This** is a good dip for Mexican- or southwestern-style wings.

1 cup sour cream
½ cup mayonnaise
½ cup chopped fresh
cilantro
¼ teaspoon (1 small clove)
minced fresh garlic

2 tablespoons fresh lime
juice
¼ teaspoon grated lime peel
⅛ teaspoon ground cumin
⅛ teaspoon onion powder

1. In a medium bowl, combine the sour cream, mayonnaise, cilantro, garlic, lime juice and peel, cumin, and onion powder. Mix well.

2. Chill in the refrigerator before serving.

Makes 2 cups.

HOT APRICOT DIP

☞ **This** is a good dip for spicy tropical-style wings.

2 cups apricot preserves
¼ cup prepared mustard
¼ cup apple cider vinegar
2 teaspoons grated
horseradish

1 teaspoon light brown
sugar
1 teaspoon onion powder
Dash hot sauce

1. In a small saucepan over medium heat, combine the apricot preserves, mustard, vinegar, horseradish, brown sugar, onion powder, and hot sauce.

2. Stir until the ingredients are hot and the brown sugar is dissolved. Do not boil! Remove from the heat and transfer to a bowl. As the mixture cools, it will turn into a thick dip.

Makes 2 cups.

BASIL MAYO DIP

☞ **This** dip is great with Italian-style wings.

1½ cups mayonnaise
½ cup heavy cream
2 tablespoons chopped fresh
  basil
2 tablespoons finely
  chopped green onions
  (scallions)

½ teaspoon dry mustard
½ teaspoon cracked black
  pepper

1. In a medium mixing bowl, combine the mayonnaise, cream, basil, green onions, mustard, and pepper. Mix well.

2. Chill in the refrigerator before serving.

Makes 2 cups.

GREEN SAMBAL DIP

☞ **Serve** this dip with Thai-style wings.

1 cup sour cream
4 green onions (scallions),
    chopped
¾ teaspoon grated fresh
    gingerroot
½ tablespoon fresh lime
    juice
½ tablespoon fresh lemon
    juice

¼ cup chopped fresh
    cilantro
2¼ teaspoons curry powder
½ teaspoon garlic powder
½ teaspoon onion powder
1 teaspoon crushed dried
    red pepper
½ teaspoon sugar
½ teaspoon salt

1. In a medium bowl, combine the sour cream, green onions, ginger, lime and lemon juices, cilantro, curry, garlic and onion powders, crushed pepper, sugar, and salt. Mix well.

2. Chill in the refrigerator before serving.

Makes 2 cups.

TROPICAL FRUIT DIP

1 mango, peeled, cleaned,
  and pitted
1 papaya, peeled, cleaned,
  and seeded
1 red onion, finely chopped
1 cup apple cider vinegar
¼ cup light brown sugar,
  packed
¼ cup black raisins
½ tablespoon dark rum

¼ cup shredded sweetened
  coconut
½ teaspoon fresh lime juice
2 garlic cloves, minced
¼ teaspoon ground allspice
⅛ teaspoon dried thyme
⅛ teaspoon ground black
  pepper
⅛ teaspoon salt
Dash hot sauce

1. In a food processor, combine the mango, papaya, onion, vinegar, brown sugar, raisins, rum, coconut, lime juice, garlic, allspice, thyme, pepper, salt, and hot sauce.

2. Blend until the ingredients are pureed. Transfer to a small saucepan over a high flame. Bring to a boil while stirring, then reduce the heat and simmer for 12 minutes. Let the mixture cool for 20 minutes.

3. Chill in the refrigerator before serving.

Makes 3 cups.

CELERY-ONION DIP

☞ **This** is a good substitute for the traditional blue cheese dip.

1 cup mayonnaise
⅔ cup sour cream
½ cup finely chopped celery
1 tablespoon finely chopped
   red onion
2 teaspoons chopped fresh
   mint

¼ teaspoon cayenne pepper
⅛ teaspoon prepared
   mustard
⅛ teaspoon onion powder
⅛ teaspoon ground black
   pepper
⅛ teaspoon celery salt

1. In a medium mixing bowl, combine the mayonnaise, sour cream, celery, onion, mint, cayenne, mustard, onion powder, pepper, and celery salt. Mix well.

2. Chill in the refrigerator before serving.

Makes 2 cups.

GRANDMA'S BLUE CHEESE DIP

☞ **Grandma** recommends this dip with very hot wings!

¾ cup (12 ounces) softened
   cream cheese
¼ cup whole milk
⅓ cup mayonnaise
1 tablespoon fresh lemon
   juice
1 tablespoon finely minced
   onion

¼ teaspoon hot sauce
¼ teaspoon Worcestershire
   sauce
¾ cup crumbled blue cheese
⅛ teaspoon onion powder
⅛ teaspoon garlic powder

1. In a medium bowl, whip the cream cheese with an electric hand mixer at low speed until soft and smooth. Slowly add the milk until smooth.

2. Fold in the mayonnaise, lemon juice, onion, hot sauce, Worcestershire, blue cheese, and onion and garlic powders with a rubber spatula, in order to keep the cheese chunky.

3. Chill in the refrigerator before serving.

Makes 2 cups.

SPEEDY BLUE CHEESE DIP

☞ **This** dip is great with almost all wing recipes, and it's good if you're in a hurry, too. Always serve it with spicy wings.

1 cup sour cream
½ cup mayonnaise
3 tablespoons crumbled blue cheese
¼ cup finely minced onion
⅛ teaspoon salt
¼ teaspoon ground black pepper
⅛ teaspoon onion powder
⅛ teaspoon garlic powder
¼ cup chopped fresh parsley
⅛ teaspoon hot sauce

1. In a medium mixing bowl, combine the sour cream, mayonnaise, blue cheese, onion, salt, pepper, onion and garlic powders, parsley, and hot sauce. Mix well.

2. Chill in the refrigerator before serving.

Makes 2 cups.

HORSERADISH WING DIP

☞ **Serve** this with Cajun-style or traditional Buffalo wings.

1 cup mayonnaise
½ cup sour cream
*2½ tablespoons grated
    horseradish*
*½ teaspoon ground black
    pepper*

½ teaspoon garlic powder
⅛ teaspoon onion powder
*⅛ teaspoon fresh lemon
    juice*
Dash hot sauce

1. In a medium mixing bowl, combine the mayonnaise, sour cream, horseradish, pepper, garlic and onion powders, lemon juice, and hot sauce. Mix well.

2. Chill in the refrigerator before serving.

Makes 2 cups.

BASIL-TOMATO DIP

☞ **Serve** this dip with Italian-style wings

*3 tablespoons chopped fresh
    basil*
1 garlic clove, minced
*2 tablespoons chopped fresh
    chives*
*⅛ teaspoon ground black
    pepper*
*⅛ teaspoon prepared
    mustard*

*1 teaspoon super-fine sugar
    (this dissolves better)*
1 cup mayonnaise
⅓ cup sour cream
*4 medium tomatoes, finely
    chopped*

1. In a medium mixing bowl, combine the basil, garlic, chives, pepper, mustard, sugar, mayonnaise, and sour cream. Mix well.

2. With a rubber spatula, carefully fold in the tomatoes, making sure they don't turn or make the dip mushy.

3. Chill in the refrigerator before serving.

Makes 2 cups.

ARMAND'S REMOULADE

¾ cup mayonnaise
¼ cup apple cider vinegar
2 tablespoons ketchup
1 teaspoon Frank's REDHOT sauce
2 tablespoons grated horseradish
1 tablespoon Dijon mustard
1 teaspoon Worcestershire sauce
½ cup finely chopped celery

½ cup chopped onion
½ cup chopped red bell pepper
1 garlic clove, minced
½ teaspoon dried thyme
½ teaspoon onion powder
1 teaspoon Cajun seasoning
2 tablespoons crumbled blue cheese
1 sweet pickle, finely diced
2 tablespoons sour cream

1. In a medium mixing bowl, place the mayonnaise, vinegar, ketchup, hot sauce, horseradish, mustard, Worcestershire, celery, onion, red pepper, garlic, thyme, onion powder, Cajun seasoning, blue cheese, pickle, and sour cream.

2. Carefully fold the ingredients together with a rubber spatula until they're all incorporated.

3. Chill in the refrigerator before serving.

Makes 2½ cups.

SALADS

PARTY COLESLAW

☞ **Here's** an important salad to make for a wing party. This recipe will serve twenty to twenty-five people.

3 cups mayonnaise	*1 teaspoon celery seeds*
1 cup sour cream	*½ teaspoon onion powder*
¼ cup white vinegar	*½ teaspoon garlic powder*
¼ cup sugar	*3½ pounds shredded*
2 teaspoons salt	*cabbage*
½ teaspoon white pepper	*2 cups shredded carrots*

1. Combine the mayonnaise, sour cream, vinegar, sugar, salt, pepper, celery seeds, and onion and garlic powders in a large mixing bowl. Mix until smooth.

2. Add the cabbage and carrots, mixing well. Add more salt or sugar, if desired.

3. Transfer to a large bowl or platter and garnish with kale or red leaf lettuce.

PARTY POTATO SALAD

☞ **Nothing** beats fresh homemade potato salad! This recipe will serve twenty to twenty-five people.

*5 pounds potatoes, peeled,
  cooked, and cooled*
1½ cups French dressing
1½ teaspoons salt
*¼ teaspoon ground white
  pepper*
1 teaspoon onion powder
1 teaspoon garlic powder
⅛ teaspoon cayenne pepper

2 cups finely chopped celery
*½ cup finely chopped red
  onion*
*4 large hard-boiled eggs,
  diced*
⅓ cup diced red bell pepper
⅓ cup diced sweet pickles
2 cups mayonnaise
½ cup sour cream

1. Cut the potatoes into ½-inch cubes.

2. In a large mixing bowl, combine the dressing, salt, pepper, onion and garlic powders, and cayenne. Mix well.

3. Add the potatoes carefully to the mixture. Avoid breakage.

4. Marinate in the refrigerator for 1 hour to let the potatoes absorb the dressing.

5. Add the celery, onion, eggs, red pepper, and pickles. Mix gently to avoid breakage.

6. Add the mayonnaise and sour cream. Again, be gentle.

7. Transfer to a bowl or platter garnished with kale or red leaf lettuce.

VERY SCRUMPTIOUS POTATO SALAD

4 pounds potatoes, peeled,
   cooked, and cooled
1 cup chopped celery
½ cup chopped onion
2 tablespoons chopped red
   bell pepper
2 tablespoons chopped green
   bell pepper
½ cup chopped green
   onions (scallions)
½ teaspoon ground black
   pepper
2 teaspoons salt
1 teaspoon dry mustard
1 teaspoon onion powder

½ teaspoon garlic powder
2 tablespoons chopped fresh
   basil
2 teaspoons celery salt
2 tablespoons sugar
2 tablespoons apple cider
   vinegar
1 cup mayonnaise
⅔ cup sour cream
2 large hard-boiled eggs,
   chopped
1 tablespoon celery seeds
½ cup chopped pickles
   (I prefer sweet ones)

1. Cut the potatoes into 1½-inch chunks, and place them in a large mixing bowl. Add the celery, onion, red and green peppers, green onions, pepper, salt, mustard, onion and garlic powders, basil, and celery salt.

2. In a separate, medium mixing bowl, whisk the sugar, vinegar, mayonnaise, and sour cream until smooth.

3. Fold in the chopped eggs, celery seeds, and chopped pickles.

4. Pour the dressing over the potato mixture. With a rubber spatula, carefully fold the dressing and potatoes together until they're thoroughly mixed. Try not to break the potatoes or the salad will become mushy.

5. Transfer the salad to a large platter or bowl. Garnish with celery seeds, parsley, and paprika.

Serves 8 to 10.

RED DEVIL POTATO SALAD

½ cup sour cream
½ cup mayonnaise
½ cup Dijon mustard
1 tablespoon sugar
3 tablespoons chopped fresh
    parsley
¼ teaspoon salt
½ teaspoon ground black
    pepper
¼ teaspoon onion powder
¼ teaspoon garlic powder
¼ teaspoon dried thyme
¼ teaspoon crushed dried
    red pepper

⅛ teaspoon Cajun
    seasoning
4 pounds small red potatoes,
    cooked and cooled (leave
    skin on)
1 cup chopped green bell
    pepper
⅔ cup crumbled cooked
    bacon
½ cup chopped green
    onions (scallions)

1. In a medium mixing bowl, whisk together the sour cream, mayonnaise, mustard, sugar, parsley, salt, pepper, onion and garlic powders, thyme, crushed pepper, and Cajun seasoning. Mix well to create a smooth dressing. Set aside.

2. In a separate, large bowl, place the potatoes, green pepper, bacon, and chopped green onions.

3. Pour the dressing over the potato mixture. With a rubber spatula, carefully fold the dressing into the potatoes until thoroughly mixed. Let the salad stand for a few hours to develop its flavor.

Serves 10 to 12.

REALLY HOT POTATO SALAD

6 large potatoes, peeled,
   cooked, and cooled
2 large onions, chopped
½ cup finely diced celery
1 tablespoon vegetable oil
8 slices raw bacon, chopped
2 teaspoons salt
¼ teaspoon dry mustard

1 teaspoon Cajun seasoning
3 tablespoons sugar
2 tablespoons all-purpose
   flour
½ cup apple cider vinegar
¼ cup water
Fresh chopped parsley for
   garnish

1. Slice the potatoes 1/4 inch thick, and put them in a buttered casserole. Add the onions and celery. Set aside.

2. In a small, heavy skillet heat the oil over a high flame. Add the bacon and cook until crisp. Remove the bacon, reserving the drippings. Add the cooked bacon to the potatoes.

3. In a small saucepan, mix the salt, mustard, Cajun seasoning, sugar, flour, vinegar, and water with the bacon drippings. Whisk until smooth. Bring the mixture to a boil over a high flame, then reduce the heat and simmer for 3 minutes.

4. Pour the hot mixture over the potatoes in the casserole. Garnish with parsley; keep warm while serving.

Serves 4 to 6.

DEVILISHLY GOOD MACARONI SALAD

8 cups cooked macaroni
2 cups finely chopped celery
½ cup chopped green onions (scallions)
½ cup chopped onion
¼ cup chopped fresh cilantro
¼ cup chopped fresh parsley
½ cup chopped red bell pepper
½ cup chopped green bell pepper

½ tablespoon salt
1 teaspoon ground black pepper
1 teaspoon celery salt
1 teaspoon onion powder
½ teaspoon garlic powder
1 teaspoon Cajun seasoning (if you like things spicy)
1½ cups mayonnaise
½ cup sour cream
½ cup white vinegar

1. In a large mixing bowl, combine the macaroni, celery, green onions, chopped onion, cilantro, parsley, red and green peppers, salt, pepper, celery salt, onion and garlic powders, and Cajun seasoning, if desired. Mix well, making sure all the ingredients are incorporated.

2. In a separate, medium bowl, whisk the mayonnaise, sour cream, and vinegar until smooth. With a rubber spatula, transfer the dressing to the macaroni. Mix well.

3. To develop extra flavor, refrigerate the salad overnight or for a few hours before serving. Add more salt, if needed.

Serves 8–10.

SPICY CORN SALAD

¼ cup fresh lemon juice
2 teaspoons grated fresh
  gingerroot
2 jalapeño peppers, seeded
  and minced
2 tablespoons minced fresh
  cilantro
1 teaspoon ground black
  pepper

½ teaspoon Cajun
  seasoning
¼ cup sugar
2 cups cooked corn kernels
2 cups diced plum tomatoes
2 cups diced red onion
2 cups peeled, seeded, and
  diced cucumber
Dash hot sauce

1. In a large mixing bowl, combine the lemon juice, ginger, jalapeños, cilantro, pepper, Cajun seasoning, and sugar. Add the corn, tomatoes, red onion and cucumber.

2. Mix well, adding hot sauce to taste, until all the ingredients are incorporated. Add salt, if needed.

Serves 8–10.

JALAPEÑO TOMATO RELISH

☞ **Use** this as a condiment with your wings.

8 ripe tomatoes, coarsely
   chopped

1 medium red bell pepper,
   chopped fine

1 medium green bell pepper,
   chopped fine

4 jalapeño peppers, seeded
   and chopped fine

6 radishes, chopped

2 small red onions, finely
   chopped

8 garlic cloves, finely
   minced

8 fresh basil leaves, finely
   chopped

1 tablespoon chopped fresh
   cilantro

Juice of 3 limes

1 teaspoon dried oregano

½ teaspoon ground cumin

½ teaspoon onion powder

1. In a large mixing bowl, combine the tomatoes, red and green peppers, jalapeños, radishes, red onions, garlic, basil, cilantro, lime juice, oregano, cumin, and onion powder.

2. Marinate in the refrigerator for 2 hours before serving.

Makes 4 cups.

REFRESHING CUKE SALAD

1 cup water
1 cup white vinegar
1 cup sugar
1 teaspoon salt
¼ teaspoon ground black
  pepper
¼ teaspoon onion powder

⅛ teaspoon crushed dried
  red pepper
1 tablespoon chopped fresh
  dill
3 cucumbers, peeled and
  sliced
1 onion, thinly sliced

1. In a large mixing bowl, combine the water, vinegar, sugar, salt, pepper, onion powder, crushed pepper, and dill. Mix until the sugar is dissolved.

2. Add the cucumbers and onion, mixing well.

3. Marinate in the refrigerator for 4 hours. Drain the liquid and serve.

Serves 4 to 6.

PEPPERED COLESLAW

½ large head green cabbage,
  thinly shredded
1 red bell pepper, sliced into
  strips
1 green bell pepper, sliced
  into strips
1 medium carrot, peeled
  and shredded
½ cup sour cream

¼ cup mayonnaise
¼ cup apple cider vinegar
1½ tablespoons sugar
¼ teaspoon salt
⅛ teaspoon ground black
  pepper
¼ teaspoon onion powder
¼ teaspoon celery seeds

1. In a large mixing bowl, toss together the cabbage, red and green peppers, and carrots. Set aside.

2. In a medium mixing bowl, combine the sour cream, mayonnaise, vinegar, sugar, salt, pepper, onion powder, and celery seeds. Whisk well, to create a smooth dressing.

3. Pour the dressing over the cabbage mixture. Toss, making sure all ingredients are thoroughly coated. Chill for 2 hours.

Serves 4 to 6.

SIDE DISHES

BAD BOYS BEANS AND RICE

2 cups dried red beans
6 cups water
½ teaspoon salt
½ teaspoon ground black
   pepper
½ teaspoon garlic powder
½ teaspoon onion powder
½ teaspoon dried thyme
½ teaspoon dried oregano
½ teaspoon Cajun
   seasoning
3 tablespoons vegetable oil

1 cup diced ham
1 cup diced raw bacon
1 cup diced onion
1 cup diced celery
3 garlic cloves, minced
¼ cup chopped fresh parsley
¼ cup chopped fresh
   cilantro
2 tablespoons (¼ stick)
   unsalted butter
8 cups hot, cooked rice

1. Rinse the beans in cold water, then soak them in the 6 cups of water for 1 hour. In a large saucepan over medium heat, simmer the beans and water for 2 hours, or until tender. Once cooked, add the salt, pepper, garlic and onion powders, thyme, oregano, and Cajun seasoning. Mix until all the spices are incorporated. Set aside and keep warm.

2. In a large, heavy skillet, heat the oil over a high flame. Add the ham and bacon, and cook for 5 minutes, until crispy and brown. Add the onion, celery, and garlic; cook for 3 minutes, or until brown. Add the parsley, cilantro, and butter. Cook for 2 minutes.

3. Transfer all the ingredients in the skillet—including cooking juices—into the pot with the beans. Mix well.

4. Remove 1 cup of beans and puree in a food processor, then fold the puree back into the beans. (This puree serves to bind and thicken the dish.)

5. Reheat the beans over a low flame, stirring constantly. Serve over hot rice with some crispy wings!

Serves 8.

SPICY SOUTHERN BLACK-EYED PEAS

1 pound dried black-eyed
   peas
3 tablespoons vegetable oil
8 strips raw bacon, diced
1 cup diced onion
1 cup diced celery
2 quarts water
⅓ cup diced green bell
   pepper

⅓ cup diced red bell pepper
1 jalapeño pepper, seeded
   and diced
½ teaspoon salt
½ teaspoon ground black
   pepper
2 tablespoons (¼ stick)
   unsalted butter
Dash hot sauce

1. Soak the peas in water overnight. Rinse and drain.

2. Heat the oil over a high flame in a Dutch oven or large, heavy pot. Sauté the bacon, onion, and celery for 5 minutes, until brown.

3. Add the peas, 2 quarts of water, red and green peppers, jalapeño, salt, and pepper. Over a high flame, bring the mixture to a boil, then reduce the heat and simmer for 2 hours.

4. When the peas are soft, mix in the butter and hot sauce. Add more salt, if needed. Transfer to a serving bowl or eat from the pot!

Serves 6 to 8.

SMOKED CHIPOTLE BAKED BEANS

1 (16-ounce) can cooked
  white beans
¼ cup chopped onion
¼ pound uncooked bacon,
  finely diced
¾ cup molasses
½ cup ketchup
¼ cup packed light brown
  sugar

1 smoked, dried chipotle
  pepper, seeded and
  crushed
1 teaspoon dry mustard
1 teaspoon salt
1 teaspoon Worcestershire
  sauce
1 tablespoon chopped fresh
  cilantro

1. Preheat the oven to 325° F.

2. In a medium mixing bowl, combine the beans, onion, bacon, molasses, ketchup, brown sugar, chipotle, mustard, salt, Worcestershire, and cilantro. Mix well.

3. Transfer the mixture to a buttered 4- to 6-inch-deep baking dish. Cover with foil and bake for 4 hours, checking the beans every hour for moisture content. If they become too dry, add a little water.

Serves 4 to 6.

HOT CORN PUDDING

2 cups fresh-cut corn

2 large eggs, separated

1 cup whole milk

2 teaspoons unsalted butter, melted

1 teaspoon salt

⅛ teaspoon ground white pepper

¼ teaspoon onion powder

¼ teaspoon garlic powder

⅛ teaspoon cayenne pepper

⅛ teaspoon chile powder

1. Preheat the oven to 325° F.

2. Place the corn in a large mixing bowl, and set aside.

3. Beat the egg yolks, milk, butter, salt, and spices in a separate, small mixing bowl. Transfer to the large bowl with the corn, mixing well.

4. In a cold, medium bowl (place it in the freezer for 10 minutes), beat the egg whites until stiff peaks form. With a rubber spatula, fold the whites into the corn mixture.

5. Pour the corn batter into a buttered 4- to 6-inch-deep baking dish. Bake for 25 to 30 minutes. The pudding is done when it feels firm in the middle and a wooden pick inserted into the center comes out dry.

Serves 4 to 6.

CRAZY CORN FRITTERS

½ cup whole milk

2 cups cooked corn

1½ cups all-purpose flour

1 teaspoon salt

⅓ teaspoon ground black
  pepper

¼ teaspoon chile powder

¼ teaspoon garlic powder

⅛ teaspoon cayenne pepper

2 teaspoons baking powder

2 tablespoons chopped fresh
  cilantro

1 tablespoon unsalted
  butter, melted

2 large eggs, beaten

¼ cup vegetable oil

1. In a medium mixing bowl, combine the milk and corn.

2. Place in a flour sifter the flour, salt, pepper, chile, onion, and garlic powders, cayenne, and baking powder. Sift this mixture over the corn and milk.

3. Add the fresh cilantro, melted butter, and eggs. Fold the mixture together; do not overmix.

4. In a heavy skillet or griddle, heat the oil over a high flame. Use a spoon to drop in fritters. When one side is brown, turn each fritter with a spatula or slotted spoon and brown the other side. Transfer to a paper towel to drain.

Serves 6 to 8.

BAKED TOMATOES IN HEAT

6 large, ripe, firm tomatoes
1 cup bread crumbs
½ teaspoon salt
¼ teaspoon garlic powder
¼ teaspoon Cajun
    seasoning
1 tablespoon minced onion
1 tablespoon minced red bell
    pepper

½ cup shredded cheddar
    cheese
1 teaspoon minced fresh
    cilantro
3 tablespoons unsalted
    butter, melted
Dash hot sauce

1. Preheat the oven to 350° F.

2. Slice off the stem ends of the tomatoes. Cut out the center of each tomato, creating a shallow cup.

3. In a small mixing bowl, combine the bread crumbs, salt, garlic powder, Cajun seasoning, minced onion, red pepper, cheddar, cilantro, melted butter, and hot sauce. Mix well.

4. Fill the tomatoes with stuffing. Place in a greased baking dish and bake for 24 to 30 minutes.

Serves 6.

PEPPERED FRIED GREEN TOMATOES

6 unbruised green tomatoes
Olive oil, for frying
¾ teaspoon garlic powder
¾ teaspoon dried oregano

⅓ teaspoon salt
⅓ teaspoon ground black
   pepper
⅛ teaspoon Cajun seasoning

1. Wash, de-stem, and cut the tomatoes in ½-inch-thick slices. Set aside.

2. In a small mixing bowl, combine the garlic powder, oregano, salt, pepper, and Cajun seasoning. Mix well.

3. Sprinkle the spice blend lightly onto both sides of the tomato slices. Set aside.

4. In a large, heavy skillet, heat olive oil over a high flame.

5. Fry the tomatoes in the hot oil until both sides are lightly brown and crispy. Drain on a paper towel.

Serves 6–8.

BUFFALO MASHED POTATOES

2½ pounds peeled Idaho
   potatoes
1 cup heavy cream
6 tablespoons (¾ stick)
   unsalted butter
2 tablespoons crumbled blue
   cheese

1 tablespoon chopped fresh
   parsley
½ teaspoon crushed black
   pepper
Dash hot sauce
Salt, to taste

1. Place the potatoes in a medium pot and cover with water. Bring to a boil, then cover the pot and cook for 15 to 20 minutes, or until the potatoes are soft. (Pierce a potato with a fork; it's ready if it slides off.)

2. Drain the excess water. Keep pot covered. Immediately, heat the heavy cream and butter in a small saucepan until they're hot.

3. Mash the potatoes in the pot with a hand masher. Slowly add the hot cream-butter mixture to the mash.

4. With a rubber spatula, fold in the blue cheese, parsley, pepper, and hot sauce. Add salt as needed.

Serves 4–6.

GARLICKY CAJUN POTATOES

¼ cup olive oil
6 garlic cloves, sliced thin
½ cup (¼ pound, or 1 stick) unsalted butter
24 red potatoes, cooked and still warm
¼ cup chopped fresh parsley

½ teaspoon salt
¼ teaspoon ground black pepper
¼ teaspoon onion powder
¼ teaspoon Cajun seasoning

1. Preheat the oven to 350° F.

2. In a very large, heavy skillet or Dutch oven, heat the olive oil over a high flame. Add the garlic slices and let them brown for 2 minutes. Immediately add the butter. Once the butter is melted, add the potatoes to the skillet.

3. Sprinkle the parsley, salt, pepper, onion powder, and Cajun seasoning over the potatoes. Shake the skillet to coat the potatoes with butter and spices.

4. Place the skillet in the oven for an additional 8 minutes, to ensure that the potatoes are hot and flavored.

Serves 4–6.

SKILLET HASH-BROWN POTATOES

6 cups finely diced cooked
    potatoes (¼-inch dice)
2 tablespoons all-purpose
    flour
1 teaspoon cornmeal
1½ teaspoons salt
½ teaspoon ground white
    pepper

½ teaspoon onion powder
½ teaspoon garlic powder
½ teaspoon paprika
⅛ teaspoon cayenne pepper
3 tablespoons vegetable oil
6 raw bacon strips, diced

1. In a large mixing bowl, combine the potatoes, flour, cornmeal, salt, pepper, onion and garlic powders, paprika, and cayenne. Mix well.

2. In a large nonstick pan heat the oil over a high flame. Add the bacon and cook until lightly brown, about 3 minutes.

3. Press the potato mixture into the pan with the bacon. Cook the potatoes over medium heat for 8 to 10 minutes. Turn them with a spatula when the bottom is golden brown. Repeat on the other side. Slide the potatoes from the skillet onto a serving platter.

Serves 4–6.

BUFFIE HUFFIE PUPPIES

1½ cups cornmeal
½ cup all-purpose flour
1 teaspoon baking powder
1 teaspoon salt
¼ teaspoon onion powder
⅛ teaspoon Cajun
   seasoning
⅛ teaspoon hot sauce

¾ cup whole milk
1 large egg, lightly beaten
2 tablespoons vegetable oil
2 tablespoons finely
   chopped green onions
   (scallions)
Vegetable oil, for frying

1. Sift cornmeal, flour, baking powder, salt, onion powder, and Cajun seasoning into a medium mixing bowl.

2. In a separate, medium bowl, combine hot sauce, milk, egg, 2 tablespoons oil, and green onions.

3. Stir the liquid mixture into the dry ingredients. Do not overmix.

4. Heat 2 inches of oil to about 350° F in a heavy skillet over a high flame. With a spoon, drop the batter into the oil, forming little balls. Fry them for 3 minutes, or until golden brown. Drain on paper towels.

Makes 2 to 6 servings.

EASY GARLIC BREAD

6 garlic cloves, sliced thin
¾ (1½ sticks) softened
   unsalted butter
½ teaspoon garlic powder
½ teaspoon onion powder
¼ teaspoon dried basil
¼ teaspoon dried oregano

¼ teaspoon salt
¼ teaspoon ground black
   pepper
¼ teaspoon paprika
1 loaf Italian bread, sliced
   lengthwise

1. Preheat the oven to 350° F.

2. In a small mixing bowl, cream together the garlic, butter, garlic and onion powders, basil, oregano, salt, pepper, and paprika.

3. With a rubber spatula, spread the open-faced bread with the butter mixture.

4. Place the bread on a foil-covered baking sheet and bake for 5 minutes.

5. Turn on the broiler and brown the top of the bread for 2 minutes.

6. Fold both sides of bread together again and wrap in aluminum foil to keep warm.

Makes 2 to 6 servings.

YUMMY BEER-BATTERED ONION RINGS

1¼ cups all-purpose flour
1 teaspoon baking powder
1 teaspoon salt
¼ teaspoon cayenne pepper
2 tablespoons (¼ stick)
    margarine
1 large egg, beaten

1 cup beer
1 large Spanish or Vidalia
    onion
All-purpose flour, for
    dusting
Vegetable oil, for deep-
    frying

1. In a medium bowl, combine the flour, baking powder, salt, and cayenne. Cut in the margarine until the mixture resembles fine crumbs.

2. Add the egg and beer. Whisk until the batter is smooth.

3. Cut the onion into 1/4-inch-thick slices. With your fingers, separate the slices into rings, then place them in a large bowl. Dust with flour.

4. Heat oil in a fryer to 350° F. With tongs, dip each onion ring into the batter. Lift the onion ring carefully from the batter, and let any excess batter drip off. (The batter's consistency is perfect when it drips very slowly off of the onion ring while fully coating it.)

5. Carefully drop each onion ring into the oil and fry for 6 to 8 minutes until golden brown and crispy.

Serves 4 to 6 as a side dish.

INDEX